W.H. Michael

Memorial addresses on the life and character of Austin F. Pike

W.H. Michael

Memorial addresses on the life and character of Austin F. Pike

ISBN/EAN: 9783741132483

Manufactured in Europe, USA, Canada, Australia, Japa

Cover: Foto ©Thomas Meinert / pixelio.de

Manufactured and distributed by brebook publishing software (www.brebook.com)

W.H. Michael

Memorial addresses on the life and character of Austin F. Pike

MEMORIAL ADDRESSES

ON THE

LIFE AND CHARACTER

OF

AUSTIN F. PIKE,

(A SENATOR FROM NEW HAMPSHIRE),

DELIVERED IN THE

SENATE AND HOUSE OF REPRESENTATIVES,

FEBRUARY 16 AND 22, 1887.

Prepared in accordance with joint resolution of Congress, and by authority of the Joint Committee on Printing,

BY

W. H. MICHAEL,

CLERK OF PRINTING RECORDS, UNITED STATES SENATE.

WASHINGTON:
GOVERNMENT PRINTING OFFICE.
1888.

JOINT RESOLUTION PROVIDING FOR PRINTING EULOGIES DELIVERED IN CONGRESS UPON THE LATE AUSTIN F. PIKE.

Resolved by the Senate and House of Representatives of the United States of America in Congress assembled, That there be printed of the eulogies delivered in Congress upon the late AUSTIN F. PIKE, a Senator from New Hampshire, twelve thousand copies, of which four thousand copies shall be for the use of the Senate and eight thousand copies for the use of the House of Representatives.

That the Secretary of the Treasury be, and he is hereby, directed to have printed a portrait of AUSTIN F. PIKE, to accompany said eulogies, and for the purpose of engraving and printing said portrait the sum of three thousand dollars, or so much thereof as may be necessary, is hereby appropriated out of any moneys in the Treasury not otherwise appropriated.

Approved, March 3, 1887.

CONTENTS.

	Page.
Biographical sketch	3
The obsequies	6
Announcement in the Senate	10

Proceedings in the Senate.

Address of Mr. Blair, of New Hampshire	11
Mr. Edmunds, of Vermont	24
Mr. Dolph, of Oregon	26
Mr. Manderson, of Nebraska	33
Mr. Jones, of Arkansas	36
Mr. George, of Mississippi	39
Mr. Evarts, of New York	41
Mr. Palmer, of Michigan	45
Mr. Cheney, of New Hampshire	49

Proceedings in the House of Representatives.

Address of Mr. Haynes, of New Hampshire	54
Mr. Long, of Massachusetts	59
Mr. Holman, of Indiana	62
Mr. Gallinger, of New Hampshire	65
Mr. Allen, of Massachusetts	75
Mr. Dingley, of Maine	80
Mr. Cutcheon, of Michigan	83

BIOGRAPHICAL SKETCH.

Senator PIKE was the son of Uriah and Mary (Page) Pike, and was born in Hebron, October 16, 1819, upon a farm at the head of Newfound Lake. He received his rudimentary education in his native town, under the instruction of the late George G. Fogg, working upon the farm in vacations, and graduated at Holmes Academy, at Plymouth, when Samuel Reed Hale was principal. He went to Franklin when twenty-two years of age, studied law with Hon. George W. Nesmith, and was admitted to the bar July 13, 1845. He settled in the practice of his profession as the partner of Judge Nesmith, and has ever since made Franklin his home.

His law partnership with Judge Nesmith continued until 1854, when it was dissolved, and Daniel Barnard became associated with Mr. PIKE, the firm being Pike & Barnard. This continued down to 1863, when Mr. Barnard retired and Isaac N. Blodgett, now one of the justices of the supreme court, became his partner, and so continued until his appointment to the bench, when Frank N. Parsons, who had married one of Mr. PIKE's daughters, was taken in as his partner.

Senator PIKE was twice married. By his first wife he had no children. In 1850 he married Caroline White, by whom he had three children: Helen, the wife of Frank N.

Parsons; Edward E., and Leila. Mr. PIKE, at the time of his death, was president of the Citizens' National Bank at Tilton, and one of the board of trustees of the Franklin Library Association.

He was always active in politics. He was elected representative from Franklin in 1850, 1851, 1852, 1865, and 1866, being speaker of the house the last two years; was elected to the State senate in 1857 and 1858, and was president of that body in the latter year; he was a member of the Republican National Convention which nominated John C. Fremont in 1856; was elected a member of the Forty-third Congress in 1873, and defeated for the next Congress. While a member of the National House he served on the Committee on Elections. On Thursday, August 2, 1883, he was elected United States Senator for the term beginning March 4 of that year, after a long contest, in which he had not been a candidate in the ordinary sense. He worked untiringly while in the Senate, holding positions on committees of importance, and was an able, dignified, and courteous Senator.

THE CIRCUMSTANCES OF HIS DEATH.

The circumstances of Mr. PIKE'S death show that he himself had no premonition of its near approach. He was at his farm, about one mile from Franklin village, October 8, 1886, in company with Frank B. Richardson, road-master of the Northern Division of the Boston and Lowell Railroad, with whom he was looking over a gravel bank which the railroad company had recently purchased. It was a very warm day for October, the sun during the middle of the day shining with almost summer fierceness, and while walking across the fields to the gravel bank Mr. PIKE frequently complained of the heat, but said nothing about internal pain or trouble. On arriving at the bank Mr. PIKE proceeded to point out the boundaries, standing at a spot where the gravel had been taken away, leaving a sharp descent of 6 or 8 feet. He raised his hand and pointed out the boundary in one direction, and as he turned to indicate the other he suddenly sank to the earth. Mr. Richardson at first supposed that he was merely sitting down to rest, but suddenly Mr. PIKE fell to the ground and rolled down the declivity mentioned. As Mr. Richardson sprang after him he lifted his hands as if for assistance, his eyes gave an expressive look, as though he realized for an instant his situation, and then his arms dropped beside his body, and all was over. Mr. Richardson carried his remains to the top of the bank, and then, summoning assistance, had them removed to his home.

THE OBSEQUIES.

The obsequies of United States Senator AUSTIN F. PIKE occurred in Franklin, N. H., October 12, 1886. There was a large attendance, and more distinguished public men were assembled than had been seen before for many years on a similar occasion in New Hampshire. Business was generally suspended during the funeral. A draped flag was suspended across the main street of the West Village, and the entire community united in paying the greatest honors to so eminent and highly respected a citizen. A service was held at the home of the deceased, on Main street, at half past one o'clock, at which Rev. J. H. Bliss read a few sentences from the Bible and offered prayer. A procession was then formed, which moved slowly to the Congregational Church near by.

The Concord Union published the following in its special report of the obsequies:

"The beautiful village of Franklin wore a mournful aspect to-day, for her most distinguished citizen lay dead. From an early hour this morning people began coming from the neighboring towns to show their respect for the dead Senator. The streets were lined with people, and the capacity of the two hotels was taxed to the utmost. Business was wholly suspended, and a Sunday stillness pervaded the community. Senator PIKE had been an inhabitant of Franklin since his boyhood; his active life had been spent in the village; he was foremost in every public undertaking, and at his decease it was but natural that those to whom he had been known so long should feel that they had met with a personal loss. His kindly ways were recounted by the people, and many were the reminiscences called forth by the occasion. It was a sad day for Franklin, and will long be remembered. The lovely village on the banks of the Merrimack is noted for its distinguished citizens, but Mr. PIKE's death leaves a great void, which will probably never be filled. This certainly seemed to be the prevailing sentiment at his funeral. But the loss is not to his town alone, but to the State as well, for his superior abilities had given him a wide reputation both in law and politics.

"The regular morning express from Concord carried up a large number of prominent people, and this was followed at 12.30 by a special train that carried many more.

"The pall-bearers were Hon. George W. Nesmith, LL. D., of Franklin; ex-Governor Cheney, of Manchester; ex-Secretary Chandler and ex-Senator Rollins, of Concord; Hon. Daniel Barnard and Mr. Justice Blodgett (of the supreme court), of Franklin; ex-Congressman Hibbard, of Laconia, and William T. Cass, of Tilton, the latter representing the Citizens' National Bank of that town, of which the dead Senator was president. The committee of the United States Senate consisted of Senator Edmunds, of Vermont; Senator Evarts, of New York; Senator Pugh, of Alabama; Senator Jones, of Arkansas; Senator Aldrich, of Rhode Island; Senator Sabin, of Minnesota; and Senator Blair, of New Hampshire, who was accompanied by Sergeant-at-Arms Col. W. P. Canaday, Assistant Doorkeeper J. I. Christie, and Messrs.

D. S. Corser and C. B. Reade. Among the many other noted men in attendance were Governor Currier and General Williams, of his staff; Hon. B. A. Kimball, of the executive council; ex-Governor Berry, of Bristol; ex-Governor Smyth, of Manchester; ex-Senator Patterson, of Hanover; Congressmen Haynes and Gallinger; ex-Congressman Ray, of Lancaster; ex-Chief Justice Sargent, of Concord; Justice Bingham, of the supreme court; Hon. Jesse Gault, of Hookset; Hon. Daniel Hall, of Dover; Col. J. Horace Kent, of Portsmouth; Hon. Cyrus Taylor, of Bristol; President Pike, and Ira Chase, clerk of the State senate; Hon. Charles F. Stone, of Laconia; Messengers H. H. Rand and C. W. Barrett and Clerk W. B. Fellows, of the United States Senate; George W. Murray and Frank D. Currier, of Canaan; Hon. O. C. Moore and Hon. Charles Holman, of Nashua; Hon. William W. Flanders, of Wilmot; William T. Norris, of Danbury; Hon. George B. Chandler, Hon. David Cross, Hon. Henry M. Putney, and Hon. J. W. Fellows, of Manchester; John H. Pearson, Parsons B. Cogswell, Charles R. Corning, Hon. Oliver Pillsbury, Hon. David F. Willard, Hon. S. C. Eastman, Judge Dana, and T. L. Norris, of Concord; John C. Linehan, Isaac K. Gage, and W. A. Buxton, of Penacook; and Hon. A. W. Sulloway, Hon. Warren F. Daniell, Hon. E. B. S. Sanborn, Walter Aiken, E. G. Leach, O. A. Towne, and S. H. Robie, of Franklin.

"The church was crowded, and many were unable to gain admittance. The remains rested in an elegant casket, with a gold plate bearing simply the name of the dead. The body was attired in full evening dress, with the arms folded across the breast. His face wore a life-like expression, and it was hard to realize that the Senator was dead. The floral gifts were many and beautiful. The citizens of the town gave a massive broken column composed of white and blush roses and carnations, the top covered with asters. The shaft rested on a bank of roses and ferns and was encircled with a wreath of ivy and a white satin band. Rare cut flowers, trailing vines, and foliage plants were also profusely displayed.

"The services began with the singing, by Mrs. R. G. Burleigh, Mrs. Warren F. Daniell, George L. Sanborn, and W. L. Stevens, with Mrs. George P. Gale as organist, of the chant, 'I will lift up mine eyes,' followed by the reading of the Scriptures by Rev. Mr. Bliss. 'The Lord is my Shepherd' was then sung. Rev. Mr. Bliss made an appropriate address, in which he gave a brief sketch of the deceased, enumerated the many public positions which he had so creditably filled, and paid a generous tribute to his nobleness of character and private virtues. After prayer the quartette sang the hymn 'Integer Vitæ,' after which an opportunity was given to view the remains. The cortege then moved to the Franklin Cemetery, where there was a brief burial service. The widow and daughters, who were not present in the church, went up to the grave as it was surrounded by a concourse of people and, after the casket was lowered, strewed it with flowers.

"The funeral was directed by C. C. Paige and Messrs. Canaday and Christie."

ANNOUNCEMENT OF THE DEATH OF SENATOR PIKE IN THE SENATE.

DECEMBER 6, 1886.

Mr. BLAIR. Mr. President, although it is already a well-known fact, I feel that it will touch the Senate with a sense of deep grief when, in the discharge of a painful duty, I announce the death of Hon. AUSTIN F. PIKE, late a member of this body from New Hampshire.

It will be remembered that shortly before the close of the last session, worn out by the struggle with what finally proved to be a fatal disease, he sought health and strength among the hills of his nativity. He thought, and his friends thought, that he had quite recovered his health, and he and they were looking forward with hope to the prolongation of his useful life, when, in a moment, in the twinkling of an eye, he was and he was not, for God took him.

At an appropriate time I shall ask of the Senate that a fitting tribute be paid to the life, the character, and the public services of our deceased associate and friend.

As a mark of respect to his memory, I now move that the Senate adjourn.

The PRESIDENT *pro tempore*. The Senator from New Hampshire moves that the Senate do now adjourn.

The motion was agreed to ; and (at 3 o'clock and 30 minutes p. m.) the Senate adjourned until Tuesday, December 7, at 12 o'clock m.

PROCEEDINGS IN THE SENATE.

FEBRUARY 16, 1887.

Mr. BLAIR. I submit a series of resolutions, and ask that they be now considered.

The PRESIDENT *pro tempore*. The Senator from New Hampshire submits for adoption a series of resolutions, which will be read.

The Chief Clerk read the resolutions, as follows :

Resolved, That the Senate has learned with deep regret of the decease of AUSTIN F. PIKE, late a member of this body from the State of New Hampshire.

Resolved, That the business of the Senate be now suspended that appropriate tribute may be paid to the high character and distinguished public services of the deceased Senator.

Resolved, That the Secretary of the Senate communicate these resolutions to the House of Representatives.

Resolved, That, as an additional mark of respect to the memory of the deceased, the Senate do now adjourn.

Address of Mr. BLAIR, of New Hampshire.

Mr. PRESIDENT : Once more the Senate is reminded that the great startling fact in life is death.

I have moved this resolution of respect for the dead and of condolence to the living because the nation has lost a patriot and a statesman ; the community a citizen wise, trusted, and efficient ; the family a model in all the domestic relations, whose loss is crushing as it is irreparable; and the Senate a member faithful, able, and beloved.

The late Senator PIKE was a man of great natural powers, the architect of his own fortunes, who from an humble though honorable beginning made his way by constant progression to the highest and most responsible stations in life.

Few men did more of hard, honest work than he, both in the preparation of his vigorous mind for the chosen arena whereon his youthful ambition determined to fight out the great combat to come and also in the stern struggle of more than forty years which constituted his active, professional, business, and public career.

Eminent in many things, and with versatile qualifications for the service of society, he was pre-eminently a great lawyer, and always devoted himself to his profession in marked preference to other pursuits. In its active practice he found an opportunity for study and discipline which largely made up for the deprivation of that more liberal and broader preparatory education upon which he entered, but the completion of which circumstances denied to him.

Perhaps the bar of New Hampshire has never been surpassed in ability and high professional character. From the organization of her government until the present time, with less than 10,000 square miles of territory, and even now not more than 400,000 people within her jurisdiction, she has constantly exhibited a wonderful galaxy of bright particular stars in that profession which has written almost every line in the legislation of freedom everywhere, and in this country, at least, has ever been true to the cause of the oppressed against arbitrary power. Her Sullivans, for three generations the great masters of forensic disputation, which they elevated by the highest forms of logic and eloquence ; Jeremiah Mason, the profoundest American master of the common law, and by the Great Expounder of the Constitution himself admitted to be the most formidable antagonist he had ever met ; the two Websters, Daniel and his brother Ezekiel, unequaled perhaps save by each other, and certainly unsurpassed in the profession to which they belonged; Jeremiah Smith, the great chief-justice of our early history, whose name will live always in the memory of the profession and no less in the affectionate regard of the people of our State; Ichabod Bartlett, quick-witted, brilliant, versatile, yet profound ; Noyes and Thompson, the tutors of Webster, whose high character and attainments were the models in the effort to imitate and equal which he necessarily became great. The Bells, who by families and generations were pre-eminent in every branch of law, in literature, and in statesmanship ; and in later times, within my own memory, a plenitude of illustrious names of whom the time would fail me to speak, whom I saw and heard and revered in my younger years, and whose high character and surpassing abilities have grown in my estimation as larger experience and wider observation of men have forced comparison between them and others who, in all parts of the country, on the bench and at the bar, have worthily upheld the dignity and administered the high trusts of the profession of law.

It was when a mere boy, toiling on a hard hillside farm, yet full of suppressed and dreamy aspirations, on one occasion when called from my labor to that most picturesque and beautiful of American villages, Plymouth, New Hampshire, which rests like a crown of peace on the banks of the

Pemigewasset, that I timidly entered the old court-house and there first saw, among his brethren at the bar, Hon. AUSTIN F. PIKE, whose decease is the mournful occasion of these commemorative ceremonies.

In those days the courts were schools of instruction. Every trial, even if the subject in controversy was trifling in character or in value, was fully attended by the people. It was a favorite saying of Chief-Justice Bell that there are no small cases. This is true. Every trial is a contest between principles which has for its object the discovery of truth and the administration of justice. Nothing is the law but the right, and a decision which involves but a penny or the slightest wrong to the person may become the precedent which controls millions or upon which may depend the liberties and lives of unnumbered citizens in future times.

In the absence of lectures, entertainments, and diversions the people thronged to these judicial contests, and there, at least far more than at the present day, they learned the laws of the land. To my youthful imagination those lawyers and judges seemed a higher order of beings, and never since, even after I became an humble member of the fraternity, have I been able to divest myself of a feeling of deep reverence for the bench as a seat of judgment and as the highest earthly personification of the work of the great Law-giver and Administrator of justice to the universe, while every member of the court who does his duty seems to me to be clothed with a direct authority in the discharge of the highest functions assigned to men.

Thus, nearly forty years ago, I first saw Mr. PIKE engaged in the active duties of his profession. He was then a young man of medium height, of well-knit though rather delicate frame for one reared upon a New Hampshire farm, with a fine head, an intellectual but resolute expression of countenance, and an appearance of steady activity, both of body and mind, which made progress continually like the advance of time.

Ten years afterwards I made his acquaintance, and have known him well during the life-time of a generation, and until my entrance upon public life, with the exception of a few years' interruption by the war, in constant observation of and frequent association with him in the practice of the profession.

Mr. PIKE was born in Hebron, Grafton County, New Hampshire, October 16, 1819. His father was Uriah Pike and his mother was Mary Page. The town is one of those places among our mountains which language can not describe in their full and everlasting beauty, but which no child who is born there can ever forget or cease to love any more than he can become indifferent to the mother who bore him.

The parents were hardy, intelligent, upright, and industrious farmers, with several children, living upon one of those hard old farms which seemed to be the natural scene of toil, yet so located amid the everlasting beauties of the heavens and of the earth, and so tempering the rough struggle upon their rocky bosoms for existence, that happy is the child who is born to tug thereon for nutrition both of body and mind.

Young Austin was a studious, thoughtful boy, who worked wearily on with the rest through the years of childhood and early youth to assist in the joint effort of the family to obtain a livelihood. Up to the age of fifteen years he had no advantages in the way of education in books, save in the common district schools of the town.

Subsequently he attended a year each the academies at Plymouth, N. H., and Newbury, Vt. I have heard him describe the great difficulty with which, by manual labor and by teaching school in the winter, he defrayed his expenses by his own work. By great effort he prepared himself for college, but when ready to enter the sophomore class his health broke down in consequence of the severe strain, and his dream of a liberal education vanished away. No one, unless he has experienced the same disappointment, knows how life is ever after a desolation. Speaking of his early struggles for intellectual discipline and advancement, he said, not long before his death:

> To aid in obtaining the little education I got, my parents were able to afford me little more than my board and clothes, but I always had their hearty good wishes, their constant and tender encouragement.

Parents and children like these have made their State and their country illustrious, and while they survive the empire of free institutions is secure.

At the age of twenty-two years he entered the office of Hon. George W. Nesmith, of Franklin, N. H., as a student of the law, and in that prosperous and influential town he dwelt the remainder of his life.

Judge Nesmith was the early and life-long personal friend of Mr. Webster, his most wise, sagacious counselor, beloved and trusted by him until his death. An able and learned lawyer, a highly cultivated and liberally educated gentleman, he was and is the very model of an honest man. His love of justice is the strongest element in a character of exceptional symmetry and strength. Beloved and trusted as no other man has been in our State for more than two whole generations of active life, Mr. Nesmith still survives to mourn for and to eulogize the man who forty-two years ago began the study of his profession under the care of so fit a master.

He was quick to observe and to commend the diligence, intelligence, and perseverance of the young man who thus entered upon active life. In three years Mr. PIKE was admitted to the bar. He at once exhibited the qualities of an active, studious, diligent, and faithful practitioner, and gave evidence of the prominence which he afterwards attained. He became a partner with Judge Nesmith, his instructor in the law, and afterwards the senior member of a firm with Hon. Daniel Barnard, now attorney-general, and when that firm dissolved, with Hon. Isaac N. Blodgett, now of the supreme court of the State. Continuing the active practice of his beloved pursuit when health and duty would permit, in the latter part of his life he associated with himself his son-in-law, Frank N. Parsons, esq., who, when health failed, assisted him greatly to carry the heavy burdens of professional and public life.

He was wedded to the law. It was impossible for him to be divorced from it. He loved it and its practice. with a love that never faltered and a devotion which never wavered. I never knew a more diligent and assiduous student and practitioner of the profession.

He was early active in political life. He represented the town of Franklin in the legislature of 1850, 1851, and 1852, and again in 1865 and 1866, during which last two sessions he was speaker of the house. He was a member of the State senate in 1857 and 1858, and was president of that body the latter year. Three years he was chairman of the Republican State committee, and he was a delegate to the memorable first Republican National Convention which nominated General Fremont for the Presidency. He represented the Second Congressional district in the Forty-third Congress, and in 1883, after one of the most extraordinary struggles known in American political life, all the conflicting and embittered elements of his party harmonized in his election to the Senate of the United States. He took his seat in this body December 3 of that year. His term would have expired March 3, 1889.

Political parties, and the country also, might oftener than they do feel grateful to that man who, by his admitted strength, elevation, and conspicuous fitness of character, presents to them a suitable candidate for harmonious and successful concentration in times of factional bitterness and distraction.

In private business affairs he was very successful, and he held many important positions of personal trust.

Mr. PIKE was twice married. His first wife was Mrs. Elizabeth Farley, of Andover, Mass., step-daughter of ex-Governor Berry, the war governor of New Hampshire, who still survives, rich in the love and honor of his fellow-citizens, and especially of the surviving soldiers of the State. This lady died in 1848, after only two years of married life.

In the year 1850 was consecrated his marriage with Miss Caroline White, daughter of Thomas R. White, esq., of Franklin. Of this union were born three children, now surviving: Edward E. Pike, who resides in Hebron amid the scenes of his father's nativity and to which he retained a never-failing attachment; Mrs. Parsons, the wife of his law partner; and Miss Leila F. Pike, who resides with her mother in the home of their bereavement.

I will say nothing of the sacred and tender relations of his domestic life, except that they were of the most fortunate character. To those who have known the strength of mind and the loveliness of the nature of Mrs. Pike during their residence in the Capital of the country or during those many years of happy wedded life in the State which they both honored even as it delighted to honor them, words of commendation or even of officious sympathy are as needless as they would be unavailing to her in the impenetrable gloom that has fallen upon her life—a gloom which defies all earthly consolation and which nothing can illumine save the light of love shining from the benignant countenance of her covenant God. She knows her refuge and her strength, and rests secure within that fortress which is higher than us all.

Mr. PIKE'S service in the Senate was performed under many disadvantages by reason of the brevity of its duration and the physical weakness and suffering of which he was the victim during almost its entire period. But it is still true that the public records bear testimony to a degree of fidelity, industry, and capacity which would have been honorable to any man in good health and in complete command of all his powers.

We know that nowhere else does real nobility count for so little as during the early years of membership in this body; nowhere else does long service merely count for so much. But during the brief service of Mr. PIKE he demonstrated that there were few, if any, stronger members of the legal profession in the Senate, which certainly contains some members unsurpassed in legal ability and that exalted personal worth which is the indispensable accompaniment of supreme legal power—for conscience is as essential as intellect to the great lawyer—than was my quiet, unpretentious colleague, who gave his rare and full-ripened mind to the difficult and vexatious work of the Committee on the District of Columbia and of the Committee on Claims.

The high appreciation in which he was held by the Senate was demonstrated by his appointment to the chairmanship of the last-named committee, on its reorganization, two years after his service began.

If Mr. PIKE could have lived and could have been possessed of the full measure of his real powers until the close even of a single term, I believe that he would have written a conspicuously honorable record for himself and for his State in the annals of the Senate.

As it is, we have reason to be proud of the much that he did and that it was done so faithfully and so well, under circumstances when most men would have done little or nothing at all. That which might have been is not undone because of any fault of his, but by reason of obstacles beyond the force of human endeavor, the supreme decrees of fate.

In the summer season of 1885 a mountain shower poured down its flood, which ran violently through the street in front of the premises of Mr. PIKE, in the village of Franklin. From the impulse to put his own hand to the work which was so natural to him, he hastened to turn the stream into a safer channel. The sudden and violent exertion either occasioned a new hurt or developed a latent weakness of the heart, and perhaps of surrounding organs, from which he never recovered.

That terrible form of disease known as angina pectoris (heart agony), of which died the lamented Sumner and many other distinguished men, fastened its unrelenting clutch upon the issues of life, and for him in this world there never more was hope. Everything that mortal skill on the part of physicians, or endurance on the part of the patient, or anxious, loving assiduity on the part of friends, or devout reliance upon a benignant Providence could accomplish was done, but without avail. All the while declining, oft-times in the throes of most excruciating torture, he labored on, smiling at pain and impending death. With him duty was the supreme consideration, and during his last session here—the first of the Forty-ninth Congress—he often seemed to me to be digging his grave with one hand while he wrought with patient industry and perfect nerve for his fellow-men with the other. He seemed superior to the uttermost pangs of disease and to the most terrible afflictions of fate. His soul power was certainly wonderful, and sometimes it awed me with a sense of the preternatural and sublime.

I never admitted to him any but cheerful anticipations, but it was easy to see that the hard sense which erred not when he judged the case of others was true in its teachings to himself. He may at times have hoped that he was deceived, but he never really believed it. He expected to die, to die instantly and without the slightest warning; yet still he worked and labored on. All must remember how, for the last few weeks he was with us in the spring of 1886, his face whitened and his step faltered and his voice grew weak, and the appeal of unspeakable agony looked forth from his deep dark eyes. He was entering the valley of the shadow of death.

I can never forget the time when he came to my desk and putting his hand on my shoulder said: "Blair, I'm going home. Brother George has kindly agreed to pair with me, and we leave to you to say when it shall be done. I'm going to the mountains; perhaps it will do me good."

I bade him good-by and godspeed. He replied to me cordially; gently we pressed each other's hands. He passed wearily through the door, and I never saw his living form again. And so the stricken Senator and his noble wife left the city for that peaceful village in the North, hoping against hope for respite, not for full restoration. The sweet and invigorating influences of his native climate, the new leaf and the song of birds in the spring time, the thrill of renewed intercourse with old friends and with familiar associations seemed for awhile to really strengthen him, and from time to time I heard of his supposed improvement, until I flattered myself that his life might be spared even for years.

Exacting engagements prevented my visiting him, when suddenly, while in a distant State, I read in the telegraphic column the news of his instantaneous death. Walking in the fields with a friend, he raised his arm and, pointing to a monument, he said, "The boundary is there." Instantly he had passed beyond the boundary of life and was in the unmeasured realms of eternity.

O, tell us, men, angels, gods, what was it that happened then! But he was ready, and sleeps in the hope of a joyful resurrection.

Senator PIKE died at his home in Franklin, N. H., on the 8th day of October, 1886. He was buried with the highest honors of the Nation and of the State, amid the lamentations of the people among whom he had lived and by whom he was loved so well, on the banks of the Merrimack, just where the cold and dancing waters of the Pemigewasset unite with those of the peaceful Winnepesaukee to form that wonderful stream which, while like all things of beauty, is a joy forever, is also, by its perpetual and blessed industry in the service of mankind, an appropriate type of his laborious and useful life.

In conclusion, I may briefly say of our departed friend that in the practice of his profession he was able, faithful, and successful. He was true to his client and true to the court. He had in a high degree the qualifications of a great judge, but though often proposed for judicial station he remained at the bar from choice. In political life he was broad, statesmanlike, and patriotic, free from partisan bitterness and the petty planning and plotting for personal or party advantage which are sometimes developed in the practical working of our form of government. He saw things in their larger relations and loved every inch of the national soil and every citizen of the United States.

As a husband and father he was pure and affectionate, a very model in domestic life. In private intercourse few men were more pleasant or instructive, and young men invariably found in him a wise and sympathetic adviser and friend. He never forgot the intense struggle by which his own career had become victory, and he was full of suggestion, encouragement, and hope for those whose success depended on the same hard conditions upon which his own had been achieved.

He was a strong and trusted factor in all the affairs of the community and of the State, and has gone to his grave amid the sorrow and benediction of that people who knew him longest and therefore loved him best.

The nation has need of such men always, and never more than now. His death, at the opening of what I believe would have been a long and most valuable public service had his life and health been spared, is an affliction to the whole country, and the Senate may well pause, even in the rapidly waning hours of the session, to pay to his memory this tribute of honor and of love.

Address of Mr. EDMUNDS, of Vermont.

Mr. PRESIDENT: There is nothing that I can add to what my distinguished friend from New Hampshire has said of Senator PIKE; and to all that he has said of him, from my knowledge of that gentleman, I most cordially agree.

Senator PIKE was an illustration, a type, an example of that New England rural life which has made New England society, in respect of its order, its liberty, its observance of law, what it is. He was a man of the people. No college or university education gave him the lead above his fellowmen, but the common school and the common rural life of a well-ordered and self-respecting farming and rural community made him what he was by nature and by education, and gave him the just force that he had in all the public affairs to which he was called; not the brilliant orator, not the ambitious politician, not the amazing and scheming statesman looking sometimes for impossibilities and visionary things, but the sober, well-ordered, straightforward representative of a people of whom he was one, of which he was a pure example, and of which he was of course a true representative.

When that same perpetual fountain that made him such as he was and what he was shall have extended to every part of the continent that the United States has to do with, and every other part of it I may say, there will be of course precisely the same result—communities industrious, intelligent, moral, religious, self-respecting, and respecting every other body and people. So I think that to commemorate in this sad, but in one sense glad, way his life and services is to pay a tribute to that pure republicanism and that pure democracy out of which I think alone can a republic subsist, of which he gives us such an example.

When I stood on a mellow afternoon of a brown October day at the side of the open grave that was to receive his body I could not help thinking of what I am now saying, what a type and example he was—merely that, and that is ever so much—of that system of social order, and of social government, and of social law which appeared in all the communities where he was born and where he lived and where he died, an example that might be imitated everywhere as the best possible for human government on the earth. The pure democracy of the town meetings that he attended, the common school education of every one of the boys and girls of the communities in which he and his father had lived, the diversification of employment, the farmer supporting the manufacturer, the manufacturer finding a market for the farmer, every operation of social industry, every operation common to all of social education and progress, every sect of religious society, every liberty of opinion, every equal respect for law, existed as a type and an example and as a progress in that community. If it were so everywhere, the number of laws we should be asked to pass would be small indeed.

So, Mr. President, as I say, I can add nothing to what my friend from New Hampshire has stated of this man. A true, earnest, faithful, patient, industrious representative of the body of a people whom he did represent has left us, and so I speak not as regret and sorrow for him, but only as regret and sorrow for ourselves that he has gone from us.

But words, like tears, on such occasions are almost idle. We do not know what tears or words mean; but we have faith, as my friend from New Hampshire has said, that there is something in the hereafter that will open our eyes to wider and better possibilities.

Address of Mr. DOLPH, of Oregon.

Mr. PRESIDENT: It was but a few months since that upon the far-off Pacific a people mourned for one they had delighted to honor, and in this chamber we were assembled in sadness and sorrow to pay the last tribute of respect to the memory of one of our number who had been called to go the way of all the earth. Since then once and again the great enemy of the human race has sent his unerring darts into our midst and stricken down the representative of a State.

Following with startling suddenness the death of him we mourn to-day came the announcement of the death of the patriot, soldier, and statesman, Logan, and again the land was filled with mourning and this chamber was the scene of the outward demonstration of a grief which could find no adequate expression in words.

Human aid and human solace terminate at the grave, or we would have gladly borne him upward upon a nation's outstretched hands. We would have accompanied him, and with the blessings of millions and the prayers of millions commended him to the divine favor.

The personal relations between Senator PIKE and myself were of the most pleasant character. Entering the Senate at the same time, belonging to the same political party, elected under similar circumstances, of the same profession, and both being upon the Committee on Claims, where we were frequently thrown together, our acquaintance soon ripened into a personal friendship, which was strengthened by an additional bond of sympathy when, upon his return to the Capital at the opening of the Forty-ninth Congress, I learned that his health was so impaired that his death might be expected at any moment.

I shall not attempt to give a biographical sketch of Senator PIKE. That duty has already been ably and well performed by another. His biography is a repetition of the history of a majority of the eminent men of this country. It is the oft-told story of persevering industry overcoming all obstacles and securing for its possessor professional eminence and political honors.

Of his record in this body I can speak, because I had an opportunity to know what it was. With his work as a member of the Committee on Claims I was especially familiar. To that committee he proved to be a valuable acquisition. His legal acquirements, his experience, and his industry enabled him soon to master the questions of national and international law which are involved in the consideration of many of the claims before Congress, and gave him great facility in sifting the truth from the *ex parte* and often unsatisfactory testimony submitted in support of such claims.

His reports from that committee bear the evidence of painstaking care, indefatigable industry, and ripe legal learning. As a member of the Committee on the District of Columbia, also, his learning and his experience as a lawyer were especially valuable. Many of the important measures reported from that committee during the Forty-eighth Congress were reported by him.

In the Senate he was always earnest, diligent, unobtrusive, independent, tenacious of his own opinion, and devoted to duty. His work was without ostentation, not calculated for show, but was of practical value to the Senate and to the country. Such men are not always estimated at their true worth. Earnest, faithful, practical, honest work is quite as necessary, not only in this body but everywhere, and quite as valuable to the nation and the world, as genius.

But, in my judgment, politics was not his true field of usefulness. His qualifications, his habits, and his tastes better fitted him for another calling, that in which by diligent attention and unremitting application he had arisen to eminence—the profession of the law. The halls of justice, largely removed from the influence of public opinion, where the unbiased mind can sift truth from error in accordance with just and fixed rules, indifferent to results, was the field in which he was best calculated to succeed.

We all know with what fortitude, notwithstanding the critical condition of his health, he assumed the arduous duties of the chairmanship of the Committee on Claims at the opening of the Forty-ninth Congress. He only left his post when, late in the session, his physicians prescribed for him absolute rest. Even then, that his work might be completed as far as possible, he sought and obtained the consent of the Senate to take up for consideration, before his departure, the bills reported by him from the Committee on Claims.

He left this chamber for the quiet of his New Hampshire home, no doubt with the consciousness that he left it forever; and all of us, I think, who were acquainted with the circumstances of his case, believed it more than probable that he would never return.

It is to human ambition and the restless activity it produces that the world is chiefly indebted for its progress.

Man is placed upon the earth for action. Toil is decreed as the lot of every son of Adam. Every one has duties to perform in the world in securing the comfort and happiness of his fellow-men and exalting the destinies of the race; but as we approach the close of life, by a wise provision of nature there is less of activity and more of contemplation, the soul gradually begins to relax its hold upon those things which in early years absorbed our attention and called forth our energies, from the struggles and contentions of life, and is attracted nearer to the Author of its being.

Such, it appeared to me, was the case with our lamented brother when he left the National Capitol last spring. He seemed to be aware that the activities of his useful life were drawing to a close, and, looking backward without regret and forward without fear, he calmly set his house in order for the expected summons which was to call him from the scenes of earth's activities.

We can not, if we would, draw aside the veil and follow him into the sacred precincts of his New Hampshire home, and picture the alternate hopes and fears, the constant solicitude, the fearful apprehension of the wife and the daughter, the fortitude and serenity of the husband and father, and at last the not unlooked-for but sudden coming of the grim messenger.

How impressive the lesson of this hour! As it is with our brother, so will it shortly be with us all.

Nature on every side with ten thousand voices proclaims in unison with the revealed Word that "it is appointed unto man once to die." The decree is universal and irrevocable. Neither talent nor station will exempt us; worldly things can not aid us; human love can not succor us.

>The boast of heraldry, the pomp of power,
>   And all that beauty, all that wealth e'er gave,
>Await alike the inevitable hour.
>   The paths of glory lead but to the grave.

Many of us are in the afternoon of life and are descending into the shadows of the evening; a few more years—possibly days—of toil, of struggle, and vicissitude, and our labors will have been ended and "life's fitful dream" will be over.

The angel of death appears to be constantly hovering over the National Capitol; his darts fly swift and thick into the ranks of the national representatives. Since the adjournment of the Forty-eighth Congress we have been called to mourn the death of the Presiding Officer of this body and three of our number, and nine times has the fell destroyer entered the House of Representatives and stricken a member from its rolls. We do well to pause to-day in the midst of the activities and contentions of life to contemplate death. It becomes us to come to such contemplation with subdued voices and bated breath, as if in the immediate presence of the "insatiable archer."

I never look upon the face of the dead or sit in the house of mourning or stand by the open grave, but the thought "what shadows we are, and what shadows we pursue," comes to me with overwhelming force. How transitory, how unsatisfactory are the prizes for which men so earnestly strive. Empty are the rewards of ambition. Wealth, power, renown, what are they when a man stands face to face with death? Baubles, which amuse for a season, as children are amused by toys.

How at that time the tired and unsatisfied spirit turns from all these things which excite our passionate ambition, and from the unceasing turmoil, the restless strife, the desperate struggle for existence, the clashing of interests and purposes, the discontent and miseries of the race, to seek something more satisfying and more enduring.

> What is life? A bubble floating on that silent, rapid stream;
> Few, too few, its progress noting, till it bursts and ends the dream.

If the soul is not immortal, then indeed is death, which rends asunder earthly ties, strips us of our earthly possessions, and sends us naked out of the world as we came into it, a great calamity. But is the grave the end of man? "Shall we go hence and be no more seen?" No; we may be comforted with the reflection that "Death is nothing but the middle point between two lives, between this and another."

Faith looks beyond the grave and inspires within us a hope of immortality. The word of God proclaims that "Blessed are the dead which die in the Lord: they rest from their labors, and their works do follow them;" "For we know that if our earthly house of this tabernacle shall fail, we have a building of God, a house not made with hands, eternal in the heavens."

Our own intuitive consciousness and the almost universal belief of mankind are in accord with the Scriptures in asserting that the soul of man shall survive the tomb. The poet has given expression to this consciousness of immortality in the following lines:

                Oh! listen, man!
A voice within us speaks that startling word,
" Man, thou shalt never die!" Celestial voices
Hymn it into our souls: according harps
By angel fingers touched, when the mild stars
Of morning sang together, sound forth still
The song of our great immortality;
Thick clustering orbs, and this our fair domain,
The tall dark mountains and the deep-toned seas,
Join in this solemn universal song.
    Oh! listen ye our spirits! drink it in
From all the air! 'Tis in the gentle moonlight;
'Tis floating 'midst day's setting glories: Night,
Wrapped in her sable robe, with silent step
Comes to our bed, and breathes it in our ears:
Night and the dawn, bright day and thoughtful eve,
All time, all bounds, the limitless expanse,
As one vast mystic instrument, are touched
By an unseen living hand, and conscious chords
Quiver with joy in this great jubilee.
    The dying hear it; and as sounds of earth
Grow dull and distant, wake their passing souls
To mingle in this heavenly harmony!

Address of Mr. MANDERSON, of Nebraska.

Mr. PRESIDENT: I can not, without doing violence to my sense of the proprieties befitting this solemn occasion, sit by the side of this vacant chair without offering my slight tribute to the memory of the genial man who was my nearest neighbor from the time we entered the Senate together, nearly four years ago.

He left his seat in this body during the busiest days of the last session of Congress, and his parting words will ever live in my memory. He told me of the severe illness at his home prior to his return to his official duties, and of his apparently fruitless efforts to regain his health.

He spoke of the wearing work incident to his position as chairman of the Committee on Claims, and how much his inability to respond to the numerous demands made upon him harassed him. His conscientious devotion to duty showed itself in his strongly-expressed regret that he must leave the only place where it could be performed in pursuit of what he feared was the unattainable. I urged him to leave, saying that in the more healthful air of his native State he would probably recover and soon be himself. He said he must go home for rest and quiet, but had little hope for recovery. Reaching out his hand to grasp mine, his final words to me were, "Good-bye, brother." It was with him the usual form of expression. The fraternal word came naturally to his kindly lips and was expressive of his generous nature.

During the Forty-eighth Congress I was a member of the Claims Committee with Senator PIKE and know with what painstaking industry he did the work that devolved upon him. He handled the law and the facts incident to each case referred to him with the skill and analytical power of an experienced and thoroughly-trained lawyer, impressing his fellows with the assurance that when he came to make his report it could be relied upon, and as a rule his conclusions could be safely followed.

His was a most kindly nature, leading him to aid the claimant whenever it was possible to do so without doing violence to his sense of right.

His opinion once formed, he was tenacious of it; not lacking in that element of conviction that must lie at the base of intelligent and conscientious action.

He had all an honest man's hatred of shams, and the only evidence of irritation I have ever seen exhibited by him was when some proof of insincerity was apparent.

I came to have a very great respect for the quiet and unobtrusive man, who frequently gave, in undertone to me, his neighbor, argument and reason for the faith within him that would, if spoken aloud, have commanded the attention of the "listening Senate."

Evil could never have been attractive to such a man as Senator PIKE. He seemed to feel, with Marcus Aurelius, "Whatever one may do or say, it is necessary that I should be a good man.' As the emerald might say, 'Whatever one may say or do, I must remain an emerald and retain my color.'"

Those who knew him in the domestic circle and in his professional life have spoken of the many evidences showing him to have been truly good. I will not speak of him except as I knew him here, during the brief time we were thrown so closely together, and my only desire in speaking at all comes from my high respect for the qualities that remain to me as a fragrant memory.

> Only the actions of the just
> Smell sweet and blossom in the dust.

The final end of all to our deceased friend came in such form that we might wish our death to be like his. Much of opportunity for preparation for the dread summons, a gradual weakening of the physical and mental powers, and then "the end all here."

Shelley well describes it:

> First our pleasures die—and then
> Our hopes and then our fears—and when
> These are dead, the debt is due,
> Dust claims dust—and we die too.

But, unlike the author of Queen Mab, who saw nothing beyond the grave and to whom death was an eternal sleep, our friend believed, with all the strength of an earnest, honest nature, in the soul's immortality.

The "pleasing hope, the fond desire," the trusting belief, helped him through all his life and permitted him to look upon death as

> The great world's altar stairs
> That slope through darkness unto God.

Address of Mr. JONES, of Arkansas.

Mr. PRESIDENT: Upon occasions like this,

> When thoughts
> Of the last bitter hour come like a blight
> *   *   *   and sad images
> Of the stern agony and shrouded pall
> And breathless darkness and the narrow home
> Make us to shudder and grow sick at heart—

All human ambition sinks into insignificance; the rivalries and resentments of active life are forgotten, and our thoughts turn to the question of the patriarch: "If a man die shall he live again?"

The one characteristic that distinguishes us from all the rest of animate creation is our belief in and our hope of immortality. And if, after having implanted within us

> This pleasing hope, this fond desire,
> This longing after immortality,
> This secret dread and inward horror
> Of falling into naught—

We are indeed to come

> To be a brother to the insensible rock,
> And to the sluggish clod which the rude swain
> Turns with his shovel, and treads upon—

Then the implanting this aspiration in our hearts and minds was a cruel mockery. If, indeed, this is the end, it were better that we had been as the ox.

But, in the language of the great Apostle to Agrippa, "Why should it be thought a thing incredible with you that God should raise the dead?" In all ages among those created in God's own image this hope has been universal. Our bat-like inability to see what a bright light reveals does not prove that it does not exist. A wider and clearer vision will reveal to us that what to us seems "disorder is order not understood." Such are the paradoxes of nature that in our weakness the brightest light serves but to blind us, and darkness may serve to widen our comprehension and reveal glories never dreamed of before.

> Mysterious night, when our first parent knew
>   Thee from report Divine, and heard thy name
>   Did he not tremble for this lonely frame,
> This glorious canopy of light and blue?
> Yet 'neath a curtain of translucent dew,
>   Bathed in the rays of the great setting flame
>   Hesperus with the host of Heaven came,
> And lo! Creation widened in man's view.
>
> Who could have thought such darkness lay concealed
>   Within thy beams, O sun! or who could find,
> Whilst fly and leaf and insect stood revealed,
>   That to such countless orbs thou mad'st us blind!
> Why do we then shun death with anxious strife?
> If light can thus deceive, wherefore not life?

The ages have given no higher or nobler expression to the hope of that hereafter which is hidden from us now by life and no expression of a firmer trust in Him who watches the sparrow's fall than the triumphant words of the patriarch:

I know that my Redeemer liveth, and that he shall stand at the latter day upon the earth:
And though after my skin worms destroy this body, yet in my flesh shall I see God:
Whom I shall see for myself, and mine eyes shall behold, and not another.

If, in the great beyond, in that existence which I like to think of as "the sweet bye-and-bye," the eternal I Am shall judge us by our actions here, by our dealings with our fellow-men, Mr. PIKE will have nothing to fear.

My acquaintance with him began with this Congress. While we came from widely separated sections of our common country and differed on many questions of governmental policy, I had been a member of his committee but a very short time before his gentle manners, his uniformly courteous demeanor, and his constant and delicate attentions to the wishes and feelings of others, had attached me warmly to him.

In the discharge of the trying duties of chairman of the Committee on Claims I never saw him exhibit the least impatience or heard him turn away a claimant except with kindness.

A devotion to duty was a strong characteristic of the man, and he remained at his post of duty during the last session of the Senate long after the increasing heat admonished him that his health required that he should seek the rest and invigoration which he could find alone in his New England home.

Fully conscious of his condition, he looked calmly and fearlessly forward, and seemed to desire nothing so much as to be found in the discharge of his duty when the expected summons came.

Surrounded by the hills he loved so well, near the beautiful village where his home was, he sleeps his last sleep; and I as his friend lay this last tribute upon his grave.

Address of Mr. GEORGE, of Mississippi.

Mr. PRESIDENT: I have not that facility of speech nor that acquaintance with elegant phraseology which will enable me to pay a beautiful or elegant tribute to the memory of our lamented friend, AUSTIN F. PIKE; but I can pay to him—and if he could take note of these proceedings he would greatly prefer it—an honest, sincere, and willing one.

Mr. President, I have not had a very long acquaintance with the deceased Senator. I can only speak of him as I knew him, while we were both members of this body.

I knew nothing of his early history, and have not learned anything of it except what I have heard his colleague in this body say to-day in the elegant and forceful address which he has just made. I can therefore add nothing to what has been said as to the events of his life.

We were both at the same time members of the Committee on Claims. Mr. PIKE first impressed me as a kind-hearted, polite, and generous man, who felt kindly towards his fellow-men and desired the happiness and comfort of those by whom he was surrounded. His gentle manner, his kind disposition, soon won my respect and then my confidence and affection. I never knew a man who on so short an acquaintance so completely captivated both my head and heart.

Observing him and his services in this chamber, I will say that the discharge of his duties as he performed them required a high order of talent, a clear head, and a sound judgment. Observing the discharge of his duties as a member of the same committee, I discovered that he was an able, a well-trained, and a well-read lawyer. I found also that he had a very high capacity for grasping the truth from conflicting and contradictory evidence. I found also that he was careful and painstaking in preparation and investigation, and conscientious in the discharge of his duties as a member of that committee. I think that after his service for a very short term upon that committee he succeeded in winning not only the respect and kind feelings of every member of it, but also gained their entire faith and confidence in the correctness and integrity of his conclusions.

Mr. PIKE, as I saw him and knew him, could not be classed with that very few who are considered by the world as the great Senators of this body. He belonged, though, to a class of Senators upon whose fidelity to duty, whose patience and care in investigating questions coming before the committees to which they belong, depend in a very large degree the successful legislation of this body.

I remember to have noticed Mr. PIKE's career as a member of this body with a little more than the interest which a mere stranger of an opposite political party would be supposed to feel for one with whom he is brought in contact. Mr. PIKE came to the Senate from the Northeast, from a State bordering on Canada; I came from the Southeast, from the Gulf; and yet, in the social intercourse and the Senatorial and official intercourse which I had with him as a member of this body and as a member of the committee to which I have alluded, I never felt but that he might have come from Mississippi or I from New Hampshire.

I regarded him in his political affiliations as a firm, a conscientious, and consistent Republican; but he was singularly exempt from the bitterness of partisanship and from that asperity which grows out of political contests. I felt toward him something in this way: that, except upon pure party questions, I had as soon consult him and confide in his judgment and advice as that of any member of this body.

I have stated my impressions of Mr. PIKE. I will not moralize upon this occasion or upon the event which we are now observing. I will only add that as far as my observation extended—and it was long enough and careful enough to let me understand him—I regarded him as an honest, an able, a diligent, and a patriotic Senator. If I were to talk longer I could not say more in his praise than I have. I regard his death as a loss to the Senate and to the country, and I feel that it was a personal loss to myself.

Address of Mr. EVARTS, of New York.

Mr. PRESIDENT: The usage of the Senate, by which, when death shall have set its seal upon the life of any of our associates, we are gathered, as it were, around the new-made grave to express with respect and affection the feelings and views which we entertain of our departed friends, however frequently it may engage our attention, should never be permitted, and is never permitted, to become commonplace or cease to be impressive. It is impossible that an association that has been attended with personal regard and personal esteem for departed associates can be suffered to end without some proper recall to our minds of what it is about him that has endeared him to us, and to us what our relation is to that common and solemn fate that has severed him from us as it shall sever all of us sooner or later from our associates.

I had not the good fortune to be personally acquainted with Mr. PIKE until I met him on the floor of the Senate on my access to the place which I occupy and have filled now for almost two years; but I had known of him as a lawyer and as a citizen of the State of New Hampshire; and as my summer home on the banks of that beautiful river that divides Vermont from New Hampshire has made me, as it were, a part of that community, it was not as a stranger that I met him, or as a stranger that he was so good as to meet me. And thus this brief period of less than two years of our association in the Senate seemed to start at once upon a familiar and recognized footing.

We New Englanders, from the narrowness of our territory, and for the greatness even, as we look at it, of our combined States, so small compared with some of the single States of the Union, are apt to feel a closer association and to pass over the boundaries of the States more readily than those who are more completely satisfied in the greatness and distinction of their individual States.

Mr. President, when we say that Mr. PIKE was born and lived and reared and died in the ordinary condition of New England life, with the value of those common possessions that we all there enjoy, and that by him they were worthily lived up to, we speak of a life that has, from beginning to end, found nothing about it that was not in its circumstances and in its traits that which we might claim as the proper outgrowth of the institutions in which we have been reared and in which he lived to the end of his life. And when I thus speak of these circumstances and conditions of the life of our deceased friend and of the lives of the survivors that I see about me representing those States of New England, I do not speak of it as at all of an inferior condition of life. If admitted the brilliancy, if admitted the distinction that belong to more conspicuous communities, it does not lack any of the essential and substantial qualities of manhood and of patriotism and all that share in the greatness of American institutions and American prosperity and American fame, which, after all, find their distinction in the individual qualities of the common people of the United States.

Nor, Mr. President, is it an insignificant course of life to have begun only with the same start with all one's neighbors, and they with us enjoying the same advantages, that one should come as Mr. PIKE came to do, rise step by step through an honorable profession to the possession of the confidence of his neighbors, and then to a share in the political life of his own State, and finally by the general consent and approval of his fellow-citizens to receive this crowning distinction of being a member of this Senate. It is not by fortune, nor is it by any incongruity that this life has thus grown up and thus been graced and honored. While it can not come to all, yet it can come to none but by qualities of mind, by labors of life, and by the heartfelt affection and respect of a community that thus his life is to be filled out.

Nor, Mr. President, is it a rightful view of a life that was circumscribed in early years, as that of Mr. PIKE was, to speak of those circumstances as in our American system of society a disadvantage—to have missed some of the opportunities of education and to have been required from the outset to be frugal and careful and industrious. It is from these beginnings and by these trainings that character and life are filled out; and it would be easier to say that when affluence and all the opportunities which life can furnish to the rich are provided for the young, career in public life, in public service, in public distinction can easier be attained. How many are there who fall by the way? How often have the harder course of industry in early life and the frugal virtues that are thus required been successful in reaching the goal, while many have fallen by the way under these affluent and brilliant circumstances who might have triumphed but for these disadvantages?

That Mr. PIKE was a distinguished lawyer there is no doubt; and that he earned from the beginning and enjoyed up to his final end complete possession of the confidence of the community in that profession there is no doubt. And when we add the fact that in this second and, if you please, larger arena of political distinction his course was of the same manly nature, how can we fail to recognize that he is entitled in the fullest sense to all the honor and to all the respect that we can pay him? And when our meed is given that here he was without any reproach, and that he was the equal of all in the soundness of his judgment, in the purity of his conduct, and in the respect and esteem of his associates, we pronounce a credit to a life that needs no greater distinction.

Address of Mr. PALMER, of Michigan.

Mr. PRESIDENT: One week ago we met to pay our last tribute to a colleague who for many years had been brought out in bold relief by the calcium light of continuous high position. We spoke then not in terms of adulation or extravagant eulogy. His services were great, his life was pure, his aspirations lofty.

To-day we meet again to pay deference to friendship, to merit, and to death, and lay our last offerings upon the tomb of another who has been called from earth.

These men represent two types who, each walking well the path he trod, met finally here and then went onward to a common lot.

On one were focalized the rays from a million firesides. His lot had thrown him amid stirring events, and the elements in him had made him the point of the wedge which split opposing forces. The other reached the same goal by less brilliant but not less meritorious methods.

It is not given to all, nor is the theater presented, to achieve the double distinction of military and forensic success; yet in all that composite growth we call society the less brilliant is often as deserving and no less hardly won than the other. Each man was a type of different forces which, uniting, blending, and modifying each other, have harmoniously worked for the welfare of their country and mankind. General Logan was a tornado modified, regulated, and guided by the civilization of the church, the school-house, and the town meeting. Senator PIKE, a product of that civilization, was the steady and conservative force born of two hundred and fifty years of love of liberty, of frugal living, of prevision of and provision for the future. The rigid exactions of his conditions and traditions have for their result the survival of the fittest in such men as he.

Born in a State fruitful in great men, he became early identified with the beautiful valley of the Merrimac, immortal in history and resonant with song.

He sprang from that stock which for two and a half centuries had battled with adverse circumstances. He drew nourishment from a soil which had been ground out by frost and tempest and sunshine from under the feet of the years. He came, possibly, of a blood which had consecrated the turf of Fort Erie and which gave its name to the lone sentinel which keeps its watch over the foot-hills of the Rocky Mountains. He came of that stock which overwhelmed Baum at Bennington and hurried Burgoyne to his final discomfiture at Saratoga. He came from that stock which poured its resistless stream through the gorges of the Alleghanies, carrying with it a new civilization of which the corner-stone was the equal rights of man.

His lot was cast mid less exciting scenes than his clansmen who went forth to new enterprise and new homes; but the part assigned to him in the parent hive was just as essential and contributed just as much to that great result which we call country. In looking over a sketch of his life, I find he was painstaking, truth-loving, and never tiring in the part assigned him.

Living in the same town where he commenced his career, he passed through the usual gradations of public trust—always one step further on, till he reached the highest honor his State could confer, without a stain upon his character, and, I believe, without a blemish on his soul.

To me, Mr. President, such a life as this is the poetry of sustained effort. Many men have done brilliant things, like Alvarado or Alonzo de Ojeda. In those cases the glamor and the romance attach to the act and not to the individual. But when a man for fifty years goes out and in before his neighbors in a town where he is known to all, and we find him always advancing in places of trust, with intermissions, perhaps, but never retrograding in the public esteem, we may safely say that this man is an entity; that he has integrity of mind and heart, that he is a solid fact, that he has filled his place, that the world has been better for his having lived. His life is a compound and a crystallization of a thousand efforts, a thousand aspirations, a thousand defeats, blending and transmuting all things into an ultimate and entire success.

Such a character, I believe, was Senator PIKE's.

We entered the Senate together, and possibly there arose between us a community of feeling born of that coincidence. I often talked with him. I observed his industry, his painstaking methods. The conscientious habits of a life-time followed him here and attended him in any task assigned or assumed.

As I look back upon our intercourse I believe the night which has since overtaken him was then casting its shadow across his pathway and that he recognized the portent.

I handed him one day a metrical version of an old Scandinavian myth, which told of a city with fair towers and crenelated battlements wherein no one ever died. He read it with great interest and found consolation, it seemed to me, in the fact that endless living did not and could not satisfy the cravings of the human heart; that even there

> One and another who had been concealing
> The pain of life's long thrall,
> Forsook their pleasant places and came stealing
> Outside the city wall;
> Craving with wish that brooked no more denying,
> So long had it been crossed,
> The blessed possibility of dying,
> The treasure they had lost.
> Daily the stream of rest-seeking mortals
> Swelled to a broader tide,
> Till none were left within the city's portals,
> And graves grew green outside.

Addison tells a story of a dweller in Bagdad who, having a vision, saw a bridge projected from a cloud on the hillside to a mist on a corresponding acclivity. Beneath flowed a deep, dark, and turbulent stream. The bridge rested on an hundred arches; the first seventy were firm and intact; the last thirty were crumbling and unsafe. An innumerable multitude was continually emerging from the cloud and struggled and jostled each other on the bridge. In the bridge were numberless traps, and through them the wayfarers kept falling, to disappear in the stream beneath. A few kept on till they reached the last thirty arches, and with trembling step faltered along amid the crumbling stone, only prolonging by their utmost efforts the inevitable plunge into the tide beneath.

This was a picture of human life.

"Alas!" said the beholder, "how is man given away to misery and mortality; tortured in life and swallowed up in death."

The good genius who had attended the dreamer told him to turn his eyes down the stream, and there where the cloud had lifted he beheld innumerable islands decked "in living green." Their like "the eye of man had not seen, nor the heart of man conceived." Moving about in radiant apparel, amid fountains and flowers, under translucent foliage which transmitted the light but intercepted the heat, he recognized many of those whom he had seen upon the bridge.

The good genius said: "These islands, more in number than the sands upon the shore, are the abode of good men after death. Is death to be feared that will convey thee to so happy an existence? Think not man was made in vain who has such an eternity reserved for him."

It is a pleasant thought to me, Mr. President, and a consolation, when I mourn our colleagues who have joined the many whose memories are dear to me, that they have gone as pioneers to that undiscovered country, and that when we fall through the bridge or slip from the broken arches into the stream beneath, to reappear, with God's help, on the islands of the blessed, we shall not be received as strangers, but as longed-for and expected guests.

Address of Mr. CHENEY, of New Hampshire.

Mr. PRESIDENT: It is with a saddened heart and under some embarrassment that I rise in this distinguished presence to add a closing word expressive of my regard for the late honored Senator from New Hampshire, whose loss from this deliberative body we all so deeply deplore. The State which he so ably represented, and the sister States which recognized his eminent worth, are sorrowful over the Providence that has taken away from us a full-rounded manhood so nearly complete in its human attributes as was that of the late Hon. AUSTIN F. PIKE. The sudden termination of an uninterrupted friendship of over thirty-five years is a personal loss that I sincerely mourn.

My colleague and others have made full reference to his early life, and I will speak of him only after he had struggled successfully with his many adversities and entered upon the active duties of his profession. The venerable Judge Nesmith, the warm friend and peer of the late Daniel Webster, was quick to perceive the well-balanced mind of his young law student. With a large and lucrative practice already established, he clearly saw the importance of securing efficient aid in caring for its rapid extension. After Mr. PIKE'S admission to the bar, at the age of twenty-six, he became the partner of Judge Nesmith, and so continued for a period of years. The law firm of Nesmith & Pike was justly regarded as among the most eminent in the State, and a young man was deemed fortunate who could gain admission into this office for legal training and study.

Through a brother of mine, the late Charles G. Cheney, of Peterborough, N. H., a law student in this office, it was my privilege to learn of the rare combination of manly qualities Mr. PIKE possessed, among which were the tender care he had for his students, his desire to excite an interest in their studies, and his solicitude for their advancement. His successful life, his recognition by his fellow-citizens, and final election to the United States Senate were the rewards of industry, integrity, kindness of heart, and large intelligence.

Address of Mr. Cheney, of New Hampshire.

In political life he never occupied any doubtful position, but was always a gallant and conservative leader, unyielding only as impelled by the sound reasoning of a clear brain and an honest heart. Before he was elected a member of the Forty-third Congress he had respectively filled the offices of the speaker of the house of representatives and the president of the senate in the New Hampshire legislature. Prior to his election to the United States Senate he had been offered the position of judge of our supreme judicial court, but declined to accept that honor.

Rarely does it occur in human existence where the exit from the finite to the infinite leaves impress of honors so complete and of a life so useful. His earthly record revealed the wise purpose of human existence, and the divinity in man was made manifest by the void left in the aching hearts of weeping friends. The culmination of life's possessions had been reached when

* * * his great Creator drew
His spirit, as the sun the morning dew.

So sudden was his death that his life had passed away without even the ministering hands of his wife and family.

We approach tenderly and solemnly into the presence of the inanimate forms of our friends, but are comforted with the hope that the spirit, although not visible, is yet near. We offer our words of sympathy to the hearts most sadly bereft, ourselves remembering "how brittle is the thread of life," and as we linger by the shore of the "shadowy river" a sublime faith in our Heavenly Father lifts the dark cloud, and with clearer vision we see the "beckoning hand" urging us on to the final reunion in the heavenly home.

Mr. President, I move the adoption of the resolutions introduced by my colleague.

The PRESIDENT *pro tempore*. The question is on the adoption of the resolutions.

The resolutions were adopted unanimously; and (at 4 o'clock and 38 minutes p. m.) the Senate adjourned until Thursday, February 17, at 12 o'clock m.

PROCEEDINGS IN THE HOUSE OF REPRESENTATIVES.

TUESDAY, *February 22, 1887.*

The SPEAKER. The regular order is demanded, which cuts off all requests for unanimous consent. The Clerk will read the special order.

The Clerk read as follows:

Resolved, That Tuesday, February 22, 1887, at 3 o'clock p. m., be assigned for the consideration of resolutions relative to the late AUSTIN F. PIKE, late a Senator from the State of New Hampshire.

Mr. HAYNES. Mr. Speaker, I call up the resolutions of the Senate transmitted to the House in relation to the late Senator PIKE.

The SPEAKER. The resolutions will be reported.

The Clerk read as follows :

Resolved, That the Senate has learned with deep regret of the decease of AUSTIN F. PIKE, late a member of this body from the State of New Hampshire.

Resolved, That the business of the Senate be now suspended, that appropriate tribute may be paid to the high character and distinguished public services of the deceased Senator.

Resolved, That the Secretary of the Senate communicate these resolutions to the House of Representatives.

Resolved, That, as an additional mark of respect, the Senate do now adjourn.

Mr. HAYNES. Mr. Speaker, I ask the consideration of the resolutions which I send to the desk.

The resolutions were read, as follows:

Resolved, That this House has heard with deep sorrow of the death of AUSTIN F. PIKE, late a Senator from the State of New Hampshire.

Resolved, That the business of the House be suspended, that appropriate honors may be paid to the memory of the deceased.

Resolved, That the Clerk of the House be directed to transmit to the family of the deceased a copy of these resolutions.

Resolved, That, as an additional mark of respect to the memory of the deceased, this House do now adjourn.

Address of Mr. HAYNES, of New Hampshire.

Mr. SPEAKER: It is peculiarly appropriate that eulogies on AUSTIN F. PIKE, late a Senator from New Hampshire, should be spoken in this hall, where he once held a seat as a member of this body. There are but few here who were his associates as members of the House. They will remember him as one who, while rarely taking part in debate and wordy controversy, still left his impress as being of superior mental mold, intellectual culture, and strength of character. He was not of those who, in the current interpretation of the phrase of the day, are "popular idols."

There was in his mien and bearing a natural reserve that forbade easy familiarity upon short acquaintance. Not that he was unapproachable, even to the humblest who might seek him, but even with his intimates there was an understanding that he was a busy man, with whom the time for useless words and social compliments should be carefully chosen. With a heart warm as the sunshine to

Address of Mr. Haynes, of New Hampshire. 55

his friends, ever ready with kindly words and assistance, even impulsive in his desire to serve those he liked, still he had none of the outward manifestations of a "hale-fellow-well-met," and for this reason was misunderstood in his social character and feelings by many of the people of his native State.

No man was honored in a greater degree with the respect due to the highest personal integrity; but few held in equal estimation for superior talents; but his natural reserve tended to the close intimacy only of those of his own choice, and the genial side of his character will never be fully appreciated except by a comparatively limited circle.

It was in the line of his profession that he achieved his greatest distinction. He fairly won title to a position in the front rank of the New Hampshire bar, in a State which has contributed to the law many of its brightest ornaments. I do not feel competent to undertake a close analysis of the special traits of mind and character which made him famous as a lawyer.

He was a close student; his industry was proverbial; it seemed as if he never tired and never rested; and he possessed a professional pride which assured the most faithful work in any cause in which he might be enlisted, for the sake of his own professional reputation as well as for the success of his client. I have thought, too, that his early and intimate association with Webster and other master minds of the last generation may have had much to do with training his powers in a direction which led to subsequent distinction.

It was, I think, his average strength rather than brilliancy in any special direction which made him a leading figure in the courts of his State. Others were his superiors in glittering rhetoric. Many had greater art to please the ear with finely worded phrases and gracefully rounded periods. In presenting his case to a jury he never got down among its members with that air of deep private confidence and personal intimacy which many advocates assume so effectively. He pleaded his cause to twelve men as though he were talking to twelve thousand; not with rapid utterance, as when thoughts are crowding for expression, but deliberately, sometimes even hesitatingly, but with great self-possession, and rarely uniting the salient points of his argument with wordy bridges of glittering generalities. His arguments were arguments in fact. There was no waste timber in them. He was not prone to address himself to the emotional side of human nature. I doubt if juries ever wept over efforts of his to depict the woes of "my unfortunate client." And yet his rule of careful preparation, his studiously acquired knowledge of law and of precedent, and the directness of his methods made him a foemen worthy of the best steel, whether before the untrained petit jury or the bench of learned law judges.

Senator PIKE had none of that milk-and-water weakness which would have deemed it an offense to call him a politician. From the organization of the Republican party he was one of its most devoted adherents and trusted leaders. But he had little of the faculty of *finesse* or taste for management of details in political movements. His was not a familiar face at party headquarters, even in the most heated campaigns. But when, as in the famous counting-out of State senators in 1876, weighty questions of constitutional law and construction were in issue, he was a tower of strength to his party associates. His services as a partisan were in the direction of his special training as an advocate of principles and measures rather than a planner and director of campaigns. He was a cabinet officer rather than a general in the party organization.

He was by no means insensible to or careless of political preferment; but he was devoted to his profession, and in its practice he found a more congenial sphere than in the race for official position. Prior to his election to the United States Senate he had been the presiding officer in both branches of the New Hampshire legislature, and had represented the second district in the Forty-third Congress. To the performance of his official duties he brought the indomitable industry characteristic of the man.

As chairman of the Senate Committee on Claims, I have heard it remarked, he gave to every case intrusted to him the careful study and critical examination which mark the highest legal training and experience. He had no slipshod or superficial methods. His close application to his official duties in the earlier part of the present Congress was a matter of grave concern to his friends. It had then become almost certain in their minds that his life hung suspended by a thread, and that prudence dictated rest and cessation from his arduous labors.

It is more than probable that he too appreciated his danger, notwithstanding that at times he expressed his disbelief in the diagnosis made by physicians, the correctness of which was soon to be so sadly confirmed. I know, and others know, how bravely he looked death in the face, and it was not until the first session of the present Congress was well advanced that he could be persuaded to leave his duties here and seek in the quiet of his home the rest his condition so imperatively demanded.

But even then he could not wholly abandon his habits of industry. The last time I saw him in life was in the city of Portsmouth, whither, accompanied by his devoted wife, he had come upon professional business; and my heart warms toward his memory when I recall his hearty greeting, his generous interest in my own personal affairs, and his impulsive proffers of service and assistance. He was in the most perfect apparent health and in buoyant spirits, and yet but a few short weeks elapsed ere the tidings came, startling but not unexpected, that he had fallen in his tracks as he stood, stricken down with a suddenness which permitted not even a parting word, only a momentary glance, and a slight gesture of the hand, which told in that swift passing his realization that the great change had come.

In my pride of section I would point to AUSTIN F. PIKE as a grand type of the native New Englander. Born in the shadows of our rugged granite hills, without special advantages or opportunities, by his own efforts and force of character he rose to fame and distinction. Starting on his career in modest circumstances and with modest surroundings, he acquired by honest methods and the exercise of thrift and industry a handsome competency for his family. His domestic relations were pleasant, his domestic life beautiful in the affection of wife and children.

The rugged strength of Puritan ancestry was transmitted in finer strain in unswerving adherence to his convictions of right and duty. But while thus firm, he was broad and catholic in his views, and in his nature appeared not a taint of narrowness or bigotry. He was honest, he was faithful, he was true in every relation.

To the coming generations may well be cited as an example for emulation the honored son of New Hampshire, who rests in dreamless sleep amid the scenes he loved so well in life, by that spot of surpassing natural loveliness where the Pemigewasset from the mountains and the Winnepesaukee from the lakes join in the meeting of the waters.

Address of Mr. LONG, of Massachusetts.

Mr. SPEAKER: I do not rise to enlarge upon Senator PIKE'S political or professional career. That matter is sufficiently touched by those more familiar with it. In that respect it is enough from me that his life was, as has been portrayed, one of faithful service and perfect integrity, and that honors were never paid to a man of more genuine worth or honest record.

I rise rather because during his Senatorial residence in Washington we lived under the same roof. Almost daily I saw him and was in converse with him, and I came to know something of the deeper inspirations and treasures of his life. To the world at large our lives here are lives of official routine. But to ourselves, as the days go by, bringing us closer together, familiarizing us with each other's faces, with the grasp of each other's hands, and with the sound of each other's voices, suddenly it comes that we are no longer perfunctory associates, but friends and companions. There is in each, indeed, the conventional discharge of his duty; but beneath that, and far more impressive on our consciousness, is the recognition of qualities that mark not so much the statesman as the man—the characteristics of the individual. Out of the unrelieved mass of the representative population which we face when we enter here there steadily emerges on us in clearer outline, each day we stay, traits of individual character, personalities of individual men, the opening of the treasures of the individual human heart, and the expression of those affections, tastes, ambitions, devotions, purposes, or ideals which make each one of us a distinct individuality, yet subtly intimate with every other. And when one goes from us, say what you will, recite never so eloquently the story of his public achievement, the one sincere chord that thrills in the breasts of those who remain is that of the regard he had won in their hearts. And the measure of that regard is the measure of the response to his memory.

In this respect I recall Senator PIKE with a reverent tenderness I can not express. From the time we both entered the Forty-eighth Congress I recall meeting, almost daily each session, a sweet, grave, benignant face—more like the picture of Rufus Choate, a son of the same granite State, prolific of great men, than any other that occurs to me. I recall a gentle, almost pathetic, smile, significant of the sweet and gentle spirit from which it sprang—a man ripe in years, delicate in health, yet suggestive of something of a certain rugged New England plainness, intent on duty, going about his work in the simplest and most exemplary way, and absolutely free from all entanglements of selfish strategic maneuver. He had not been long enough in the Senate to take, if ever he would have taken, foremost part in its greater questions and debates. But there was the most diligent, painstaking, careful, and thorough attention to the details of the cumulative work which the chairmanship of his laborious committee threw upon him. To this work he brought not only patience and assiduity, but a sound judgment, an intelligent comprehension, and the trained mind of a good lawyer and a wise man. Of such a character it may seem a little thing in the way of eulogy—but to me, who was near him, it is a very grateful thing—to recall the simple genuineness of the man's nature—even the kind tones of his voice, his encouraging interest in younger men, and the gracious words to children which, together with a certain benignity in his face, drew them to him. It is a grateful thing to remember that, among all who came into companionship with him, there was an unspoken but unquestioned recognition of him as a true man, an honest man, a good man, with all that those fundamental terms mean ; that to all who came to him in his official relation, no matter how humble the applicant or small the petition, there was a genuine response; and that if one may touch the sacred altar of the domestic circle, he was its very benediction !

By reason of an affection of the heart his life was continually trembling in the most sensitive balance. And if I dwell on these personal traits, it is because he seemed to me to be conscious all this time that the angel of death walked at his side, ready at any moment to take his hand and lead him away; and that with that consciousness there came to him not only the brave spirit of resignation, but the braver spirit of doing his duty to the last—to the last letting only sunshine radiate from his face, only helpfulness from his hand. When our friends die we say, God rest their souls. But God rested his while he yet lived in the very face of death. No soldier ever faced it in the sudden and soon-over flash of battle more heroically than did he, with a serenity that was proof against its more appalling, because constant and silent, close impendence.

It was the fitness of poetic justice that, not here in Washington, but in his own New Hampshire home, death claimed him; amid the incomparable beauty and glory of the New Hampshire autumn sunshine—in the open air of that paradise of mountain and forest and lake and farm and field to which every New Hampshire heart is loyal, and on the acres won and cultivated by his own hand. There, as peacefully as his own blameless life had run, as serenely as his kind face beamed, came the end. The angel, who is even tenderer and gentler than her sister Sleep, had indeed walked at his side so long that he recognized her as the blessed angel of man's succor and peace. She had waited till their walk that bright day over the pleasant fields and under the blue sky gave the opportunity happiest for her and for him. Then she gathered her arms about him. His head fell upon her shoulder even as he went. And lo! he was at rest in the mansions of his Father's house.

Address of Mr. HOLMAN, of Indiana.

Mr. SPEAKER: The gentlemen who enjoyed an extended acquaintance with Senator PIKE have spoken in appropriate terms of his public services and personal worth. I can only speak of Senator PIKE from a limited acquaintance; but limited as it was it so impressed me with his excellent qualities of head and heart that I was deeply grieved at the announcement of his death.

Address of Mr. Holman, of Indiana. 63

My acquaintance with Senator PIKE was very slight during his service in this House in the Forty-third Congress, but I became better acquainted with him after he came to the Senate and met him daily for many months.

Senator PIKE did not seem to me to be specially wedded to public life or devoted to politics; but he was a gentleman of positive convictions, tenacious of his opinions, and well informed in the public affairs of our country and the current intelligence of the age. He impressed me as being more a lawyer than a politician; more devoted to the science of law than to the wider field of statesmanship. I observed that he uniformly took a judicial view of public measures, respected usage and precedent, and was little controlled by the demands of expediency. He loved his own section of the Union, was proud of his native State and the grand historic events associated with its mountains and valleys, and yet he took a broad and comprehensive view of the duties of a Senator of the United States.

But I was especially impressed with the moral qualities he displayed. He was a conscientious and honest man, a lover of justice and truth. He was a pleasant, unassuming gentleman, as considerate and approachable, I am sure, when here as a Senator, as little affected by official dignity, as when at home among his old friends in the Granite State. He listened patiently to the stories of disappointment and grief so often poured into the ears of Senators and Members of this House by the unfortunate, who, hoping against hope, urge year after year real or imaginary claims against the Government, or struggle to obtain or retain places in the great Departments. They touched his sympathies and often secured his best efforts for relief. He was a kind, considerate, merciful gentleman, who did not forget in his exalted station as Senator the right of the poor and unfortunate to a hearing and to justice and relief.

While Senator PIKE was not particularly wedded to public life, yet he devoted himself with unusual fidelity to his public duties. He had qualities that made him eminently respectable as a Senator. The unassuming dignity, the love of justice, the high sense of public duty which recognized the claims of the friendless and unfortunate as equally entitled to just consideration as the great demands of the powerful, which distinguished Senator PIKE, were qualities of which any State might well be proud in her Senators; and yet, while Senator PIKE filled well his place in the Senate and performed the duties of that high position with fidelity, it seemed to me that in his domestic and social relations he found his chief enjoyment. He loved his friends, and he was devoted to his excellent wife and affectionate children.

It became apparent to his friends during the last session of Congress that he was suffering from a fatal disease; that his life was ebbing slowly but surely away. I think he was fully conscious of the fact, but while his strength permitted he continued in the cheerful performance of his Senatorial duties. As his strength failed he longed for the accustomed scenes of his native State and the sight of his home and the voices of the friends of his youth, and with his devoted wife and daughter he left this capital in the midst of his career as Senator, left it never to return. The State of New Hampshire has lost a faithful servant, the nation a just and upright Senator. A good man is dead. Peace to his ashes; a tear to his memory.

Address of Mr. GALLINGER, of New Hampshire.

Mr. SPEAKER: Death is a necessary and inevitable condition of life, and before its mandate all classes and conditions of men must bow; yet, strange as it may seem, no one is ever fully prepared for the summons. "Life is sweet," and life's duties and cares so engross the mind as to keep it unprepared for the great change that sooner or later comes to every human soul. Surrounded by loved ones, in the enjoyment of home and of the tender associations that have grown around him through a life-time of struggle and toil, what wonder is it that the man of mature years still wants to live to enjoy the fruits of his labors. And yet death comes as "the liberator of him whom freedom can not release, the physician of him whom medicine can not cure, and the comforter of him whom time can not console." Or, as Swift expresses it: "It is impossible that anything so natural, so necessary, and so universal as death should ever have been designed by Providence as an evil to mankind."

And as death is universal, so, too, is sorrow. When our own homes are invaded and our own hearts desolated—when death comes to us like "the flight of some poor bird across some dark cliff, over some narrow valley, for awhile sunlight falls on its wings, a moment more and all is dark again"—we are apt to feel that our grief is exceptional and our sorrow greater than that of others. But it is not so.

In the beautiful poem, "The Light of Asia," it is told that the good Lord Buddha was wandering on the earth, helping the poor and sorrowful as our blessed Lord used to do, when he met a fair young mother with her little dead baby in her arms. And she could not believe her baby dead, and begged the holy man to give her or tell her where she could find some remedy to bring the light to his eyes and the color to his cheeks. Buddha lifted the cloth tenderly from the little face, saw that the baby was indeed dead, and then said to the mother: "Go into the town yonder with this little cup and fill it with mustard seed, but the seed must only come from houses in which no one has died." And she went eagerly away, only to return at sundown with an empty cup. All had been willing to give, but all had lost some friend. Then Lord Buddha said: "This is the only balm I had to give thee. Yesterday thy baby slept dead upon thy breast; to-day thou knowest that the whole world grieves with thee; perchance the knowledge of this universal suffering may make thy sorrow less." And, while it did not take away the dull ache, it did cause her heart to turn lovingly and helpfully towards the sad and suffering, and in soothing their grief her own grew less.

Lord Buddha's lesson of universal sorrow and universal sympathy is what I would bring to the hearts of those who mourn the loss of him whose memory we would embalm in words of fitting eulogy to-day.

AUSTIN FRANKLIN PIKE was born in Hebron, N. H., October 16, 1819. He was one of New Hampshire's ablest and best men. From very humble beginnings, and with a comparatively limited education, by indomitable energy and remarkable industry he worked his way up to the very head of his profession, and to membership in the highest legislative body in the world.

He was the son of a farmer, and at the age of fifteen had only the limited means of knowledge that the district school afforded. Then he attended a year each at the academies at Plymouth, N. H., and Newbury, Vt., boarding himself because of his scanty means, his limited expenses being met by the proceeds of teaching during the vacation periods. He often spoke of his early struggles for an education, saying that his parents could only give him his time and clothes, but that he always had their hearty good wishes and their kind and loving encouragement. After leaving school Mr. PIKE entered the law office of Hon. George W. Nesmith, in the town of Franklin, where he ever afterward resided.

Judge Nesmith is a man of remarkable integrity and accomplishments, and under his direction the young student made rapid progress in his studies. Franklin is but two miles from the place where Daniel Webster was born, and but three miles from the farm this noted man owned and occupied during a considerable part of his eventful public career. Judge Nesmith and Mr. Webster were devoted friends, and through a long period of years Mr. PIKE came in frequent contact with Mr. Webster, for whom he had a great admiration, and he enjoyed nothing better than to relate incidents in the life of this illustrious statesman.

At the age of twenty-six Mr. PIKE was admitted to the bar, and soon gained prominence and distinction in his profession, being regarded as a safe counselor and a remarkably strong and able advocate. As my colleague has said, he was not a brilliant man, but he was diligent and conscientious in his work, and always true to his client. While not possessed of great oratorical gifts, he had a sturdy strength and force of argument that carried conviction to those who listened to his well chosen words, and he soon became known as one of the most successful lawyers of the State, a reputation he held until the day of his death.

Mr. PIKE became interested in political affairs in early life. In the years 1850, 1851, and 1852 he was elected to the State legislature, where he was recognized as a strong debater and leading member. In 1857 and 1858 he was a member of the State senate, being president of that body the latter year. He was again elected to the State legislature in 1865 and re-elected the next year, serving with great ability as speaker both those years. In 1858, 1859, and 1860 he was chairman of the Republican State committee, and in the latter year was a delegate to the Republican National Convention at Philadelphia, which put in nomination General John C. Fremont, to whom the electoral vote of New Hampshire was given in that memorable contest. Mr. PIKE was an earnest and uncompromising Republican, but singularly free from partisan bitterness or political prejudice.

Mr. PIKE represented the Second Congressional district of New Hampshire in the Forty-third Congress, and although suffering from illness much of the time he made a record for intelligent and faithful service, and was recognized by his colleagues as a man of marked ability and rare legal attainments. From the close of that Congress until 1883 he attended to his professional work, but in that year, after a political struggle unparalleled in the history of the State, he was elected to the United States Senate for a term that will expire March 4, 1889. It soon became evident to Mr.

PIKE'S friends that he was in declining health, and when it was known that he had angina pectoris little hope was entertained of his recovery.

In May last he came from the Senate Chamber to the House, and, seated at my side, with a pathos and tenderness that will never be forgotten, said that he was going to his New Hampshire home, where he hoped, from the invigorating air and out-door exercise, to regain renewed strength and energy. With a slow and measured step he left the House, and on the next day he started for his home, never to return to the Senate. The fitting words of eulogy that were spoken there one week ago eloquently testify to the hold he had gained upon the respect and confidence of his Senatorial associates.

In every position to which Mr. PIKE was called he acquitted himself with great distinction. His profound knowledge of law and habits of industrious research made him an exceedingly valuable man for the public service. His clear and analytical mind, and conscientious desire to act justly toward all, peculiarly qualified him for the chairmanship of the Committee on Claims, which he held in the Senate, and which he filled with rare fidelity. It has been said of him that he brought to the consideration of claims before his committee the same degree of earnestness and the same careful research that he would have employed had it been an important case to be tried before a jury.

Even when he was suffering extreme pain he would go to his committee room and patiently examine claims, sifting the evidence and applying to each case the strong tests of his judicial mind. The amount of work he performed during the winter of 1886 was really marvelous, much of which must have been done during hours of physical suffering and mental anxiety.

The domestic life of Mr. PIKE was more than ordinarily happy. He was twice married, his second wife and three children surviving him. His home was a beautiful one, where his friends always received a cordial welcome, and where many public men shared his hospitality. He was happy in his home, devoted to his family, and true to his friends. Those who were nearest and dearest to him may well say:

> The dusky strand of death, inwoven here
> With dear love's tie, makes love itself more dear.

On the 8th day of October last Mr. PIKE went a short distance from his home to show to an intended purchaser a piece of land he owned. On that very day I inquired of his son-in-law and business partner the condition of the Senator's health, and the reply was: "He is much better, and is thinking of trying a case in court soon." At that very moment Senator PIKE was dead! Reaching the field, and raising his hand to point out its limits, he passed the boundaries of time and entered the limitless realms of another world. His death was instantaneous. In the twinkling of an eye life's anxieties and duties were forever laid aside, and the gates of eternity opened to receive his spirit.

> Low was the message that called him away,
> Swift as the thought of a child in its play,
> And in the grandeur of silence he lay,
>   Dropped dead!
>
> What did he whisper, O poet, to thee?
> Joys of an infinite glory to be.
> Dreams of a soul by the shadowless sea,
>   Dropped dead!

Address of Mr. Gallinger, of New Hampshire. 71

Mr. Speaker, for the twelfth time in the life of this Congress we have paused from the business of legislation to speak words of loving appreciation of our dead associates. The Vice-President of the United States, three Senators, and eight Representatives have passed away since the beginning of the Forty-ninth Congress. The list is an unusually long one, and serves to call our thoughts vividly to the uncertainty of life, the certainty of death, and the great question of immortality. They were all good and true men, and loving friends and associates have told, in fitting words, the story of their fidelity and work. Among them all no man possessed a larger measure of unostentatious goodness and genuine graciousness than him in whose memory our words are spoken to-day.

In this winter time of the North the grave of AUSTIN F. PIKE is covered with a thick mantle of snow, but soon the balmy days will come and the beautiful spring flowers will blossom over it—the anemone and the violet—shedding their fragrance on the air. In the hearts of the bereaved ones in the home he so recently left is the cold chill of poignant grief; but in the reunion in a better world will be compensation for the sorrow and the tears that death inevitably brings. They have to-day consolation in the thought that the life-work of him whom they mourn was made up of noble endeavor, honest effort, and conscientious fulfillment, and that among his associates in the Senate he is remembered as a man of ability, industry, integrity, and spotless life.

New Hampshire will greatly miss him, but his memory will be enshrined in the hearts of her people, and his fame be added to that of the galaxy of great names that adorn her history, and in the years to come the faithful service he rendered his State and the Nation will be regarded as the most precious legacy that he could possibly have left behind him.

The form and face of AUSTIN F. PIKE we shall see no more. His soft and plaintive voice is forever hushed. His anxieties and ambitions are alike over, and his busy life is exchanged for repose and rest. But it must not be forgotten that

> There is no death;
> The stars go down to shine on a fairer shore,
> And bright in heaven's jeweled crown they shine forever more.

When life has been truly lived; when we can look upon the grave of a dead friend and feel that the years he spent on earth were not in vain; when we know that to him "Life, death, and that vast forever was a grand, sweet song," it helps to lift us out of the rut of our own weakness, and to enable us to say, "So teach us to number our days that we may apply our hearts unto wisdom." And happy will it be for us all if when the dread summons comes we can meet the great change with the same calmness and uncomplaining gentleness that marked the last days of the dead Senator.

Address of Mr. BROWN, of Pennsylvania.

Mr. SPEAKER: I believe there will be a general agreement by all who speak to-day of the character of AUSTIN F. PIKE that he was a man who felt profound concern for the Republic. There was that anxiety and that purpose written in his face which told the world that he was desir-

Address of Mr. Brown, of Pennsylvania. 73

ous of serving his constituency for their good and for the good of the whole people. My acquaintance with Mr. PIKE began when I first came to the Congress in 1883, and I became at once better acquainted with him than with any other New England Senator. I soon felt that I might approach him with greater ease and confidence than any other Senator with whom I had business relations or friendly intercourse.

The story of Senator PIKE is one that has been a thousand times told in the history of successful men in this country. He was the son of a farmer, reared in New England and among the hills of New Hampshire, where a struggle was then required to make a start in the world. His father was poor, and all the children were taught to labor. Among those in this frugal family who became ambitious to make himself felt in society and in the community was young AUSTIN. He early manifested a desire to obtain an education, and he was not only willing to be sent to school, but he was willing to pay his own way while he was in school. That is a good indication in any boy. I have yet to note the career of a boy who grew up with an earnest desire to improve his mind who did not, if he possessed moral worth, in after life make himself felt wherever he went. It is the boy who goes grudgingly to school, or the boy who is unwilling to sacrifice for what he may acquire in school, who is quite likely to fall out by the way when he enters upon the real conflict of life.

AUSTIN F. PIKE was blessed with the noble ambition of which I have spoken. Like many a farmer's boy, when he first entered a court-room he was fascinated, and he early resolved to make the law his profession. Having once settled upon a course, he held to his resolution with unwavering determination all through life. Whatever he did in the way of politics, or in any other field outside of his chosen profession, was merely incidental and a surrender of his own to the people's will. The law was his calling, his business, to the end of his life, and, as a matter of course, he was successful.

Success in the law, as in any other vocation, depends more upon the vigilance, the energy, and the determination of the man than on intellectual endowments. To become a good lawyer demands work—hard, continuous drudgery, and that is what AUSTIN F. PIKE did throughout his career. But I knew him less as a lawyer than as a man. It was my good fortune to know him in his home life, as we learn of each other here in Washington. That knowledge of him left in my mind the impression so aptly described by the gentleman from Massachusetts [Mr. Long], and when that gentleman had described the characteristics of the dead Senator, as developed among those he met in social and familiar intercourse, I felt that he had said exactly what I desired myself to say.

I, too, had observed that kindly expression in his eyes and in his whole bearing which invites approach and confidence. It was this that drew me toward him at once, and soon I felt proud that I was permitted, as I believe I was, to number myself among his friends. It seemed to me that Senator PIKE always felt much more concern as to how he should live than as to how or when he should die, though he must have known and felt that death was very near. The anxiety that clouded the brow of his beloved wife in this regard never appeared in the face of AUSTIN F. PIKE.

He was concerned only in acting well the present hour. He was concerned for the fortunes of the Republic, and I think I never knew a man who manifested greater anxiety that our legislation here should be to the credit of the Congress and for the weal of the State.

Whatever may be said of others, we know it is true of Senator PIKE that he was here with an honest and high purpose to do his duty to the constituency he immediately represented, and at the same time to enhance the glory of the whole country.

Because he had honorable ambition in his boyhood, because out of his early struggles he compelled success, because he was true to his calling and faithful to its obligations, because he served his country with sincere devotion to her interests, and because of his kindly nature, generous heart, and Christian manhood, I shall hold sacred the memory of AUSTIN F. PIKE.

Address of Mr. ALLEN, of Massachusetts.

Mr. SPEAKER: I should feel guilty of a lack of respect to the memory of an old friend of my father were I to neglect this opportunity of saying a few words, to express, in a poor way, I am sure, the great respect in which Senator AUSTIN F. PIKE was held by all who came in contact with him, either in his professional life or in his official capacity. So close have always been the relations between our New England States, from those stirring days when the foundations of our great Republic were being laid, when the men of those States stood shoulder to shoulder in the great struggle for human rights and legal representation, down through the varying fortunes of the nation, the boundary lines have been purely imaginary, and the most conspicuous men have been regarded as New Englanders more than as representing any particular State. So it is that Senator PIKE was widely known in certain parts of Massachusetts, and wherever known his conspicuous qualities brought respect and esteem.

The barren soil, the cold fogs and east winds, the short and uncertain seasons of the somewhat inhospitable New England climate, while they seem at times to nourish a somewhat frosty and forbidding exterior, yet they have done much to build up a sturdy independence and undying love of country, of respect for laws and obedience to authority; and from nowhere more than those beautiful blue hills and rugged mountains of New Hampshire have sprung a race of men whose devotion to principle, whose love of justice, whose unyielding allegiance to their country, has done much to lay strong and deep the foundations upon which our most enduring structures of civil liberty have been reared.

Of such a race was Senator PIKE. Reared to habits of industry, thrift, and prudence; with wonderful activity and perseverance; denied most of the aids now deemed essential, he boldly carved for himself, and by his own efforts, a name and a fame which will long be cherished and respected not alone in the State to which he belonged, but by the nation as well, to whose welfare his last and ripest years were given.

He brought to his official duties in Washington a wonderfully well-equipped mind, stored with a rich and varied scholarship, disciplined by years of constant active work, worn smooth by attrition with the great minds which shine in the list of men who have made the bar of New Hampshire a wonderful record of historic names. Possessing a fund of common sense and sound judgment which stood him in good stead in dealing with the diversified questions which continually challenged his attention, his reports and arguments, and his official papers, as they appear from time to time, all bear witness of hard work and earnest thought, ripe scholarship, and a profound and exhaustive knowledge of the subject he had in hand. With all these intellectual qualities, he had, in addition, a simple sincerity of purpose and an honest effort to do just what was best for his country. Bounded by no narrow or partisan purposes, his conclusions came to command the confidence of all.

In his firm convictions, his devotion to his work, his heroic belief in the present greatness and the grand future of his country, in his unyielding devotion to the true principles of civil government, his life seems to have been a "light to the feet" indeed, in these often-time days of groping and feeling about in the uncertain ways of doubtful legislation. He reminds one of that family of patriots of old, who, once having set their faces to the sun, found no duty too severe, no hardship too great to bear, which should turn them aside in the least degree from the line of progress they had marked out, and which was to lead to the building up on this continent the free Republic which we to-day enjoy.

To him public office brought great responsibilities and duties, yet he never shirked them. The business of national legislation was but the town meeting exemplified in its widest application. Such men are rare in this or any land, and with his generation are passing away a race of men who, by their example of industry and perseverance, their rising to success over obstacles apparently insurmountable, have served and will continue to serve as an example and inspiration to us all. We do well to-day to turn aside from the bustle and activity of this life of great earnestness to contemplate, as we pass along, this figure of an honest and upright man. With his simple manners and intense earnestness he could not fail to impress all with his sincere purpose to serve his State and his country to the best of his ability. New Hampshire has many names upon her historic roll which shine with great brilliancy, but among them all none shall be found written in firmer characters or shining with a steadier light than the name of her late Senator, Austin F. Pike.

We speak of him as gone, but where? After all, how great are the limitations of human knowledge. We mourn the dead when we should rejoice; in our selfishness our own loneliness bids us mourn our own loss while we forget the gain.

How little we know. We stand on the bridge at moonlight and watch the beautiful glimmer of the water, when suddenly from out the shadow skims a boat; we catch the sheen of the light on the oars as they rise and fall; for a brief moment the boat moves across the moon-lit path and is gone beyond our sight into the shadow on the other side, yet if we listen intently we still think we hear the measured beat of the oars. The boat has gone from our vision; yet we know it is speeding its onward way. We recline at length on some sun-lit summer day and watch the fleecy clouds chase each other across the blue sky; we see a bird fly from the woods on yonder side and with joyous note speed its flight over our head. We see it only long enough to catch the color of its plumage, to hear its song, and it is gone from our sight into the cover beyond, yet we know, though we see it not, that it is winging its way to its home beyond. So is it with those we love. They are with us a day, to bless us with their sunshine and their song, and are gone; yet perhaps sometimes we can catch the music of celestial notes which remind us of the lingering harmony of their lives, and we know they have not been given us for naught.

Rather let us think of them not as lost, as ended, but just as the early morning star, twinkling and sparkling in wonderful brilliancy, charms and delights us; yet, as we watch in wonder, the first flush in the east of coming dawn causes its brilliancy to fade and fade away until it disappears from sight in the glorious beauty of the rising sun. So it is with these noble characters. They are not gone when we lose sight of them, but like the morning star, though lost to our sight, yet in their beauty and usefulness they are glittering and sparkling to delight and make bright the darkness elsewhere.

When Senator PIKE passed away the nation suffered a great loss. But if we profit by the life he lived and the example he bequeathed us we shall all be better and stronger men. And now his body rests in that beautiful town in New Hampshire by the falls of the Pemigewasset, whose eternal music shall sing the song of rest and quiet. About his tomb arise the mountains he loved so much, and whose cool breezes soothed and comforted him—mute monitors, in their bold and rugged beauty, to the character he represented. And when about those hills the evening sun shall cast its wondrous shadows, lingering about them, so shall the soft memory of his virtues linger like these twilight hues.

"Mark the perfect man and behold the upright, for the end of that man is peace."

Address of Mr. DINGLEY, of Maine.

Mr. SPEAKER: I had no personal acquaintance with Mr. PIKE until he took his seat in the Senate as Senator from New Hampshire. From that time, however, circumstances brought me much in association with him, and the longer I knew him the more highly I esteemed him.

Senator PIKE'S position as chairman of the Claims Committee of the Senate, before whom I was called upon to appear in several cases, gave me an opportunity to appreciate his practical ability, industry, good common sense, and fitness as a legislator. I am sure that if his failing health had not compelled him to avoid as far as possible the excitement of parliamentary labors he would have taken a very prominent position in the Senate. But even with the drawback of ill-health he impressed himself on his colleagues in the Senate as a legislator of great merit.

For the last two years of Senator PIKE'S service in the Senate I lived under the same roof with him in this city, and came to know him intimately. His fine social qualities, his charming frankness, his kindness, his elevated principles, and his solid and substantial character made him respected and loved. He was a type of that strong New England character which has impressed itself on the nation and so largely molded our institutions.

If it be true, as I have no doubt it is, that the physical features of a country have a large influence in shaping and determining the character of its people, then I can understand how it has happened that New Hampshire has given to the nation so many men of the strong, sterling character of Senator PIKE. On my way to and from Old Dartmouth, my *alma mater*, I have often paused to admire the grandeur and beauty of the natural scenery opened to view from a point in the town of Franklin, where Mr. PIKE resided, and in the neighborhood of which was born and reared the greatest statesman which this country ever produced—the great expounder of the Constitution, Daniel Webster. In one of his speeches Webster has eloquently described the grandeur of mountain and the beauty of intervale and river; but even the matchless rhetoric of that unrivaled master of language fails to do justice to the scene. No wonder that such physical surroundings have molded men of strong character.

In the last few months of Senator PIKE'S life—perhaps before—he came to realize that the heart disease which was preying upon him was soon to bring to an end this mortal life. On one occasion he intimated to me that he knew he was approaching the end, and that death might come suddenly and unannounced. He seemed to live in the conviction that every day might be his last. But, although realizing that he was facing death every hour, he did not seem to lose any of his accustomed cheerfulness.

The abiding faith which he possessed that this life is only the vestibule of a life beyond—that all that is real and valuable, the soul, is immortal—seemed to sustain and support him day by day. To him the lines of America's greatest poet seemed but a faint embodiment of the grand truth proclaimed by the Gospel:

> There is no Death! What seems so is transition;
> This life of mortal breath
> Is but a suburb of the life elysian,
> Whose portal we call Death.

Some would-be wise men—but oh! how weak—tell us that there is only a foolish myth in the faith which looks forward to a life beyond this which will never end; only an idle dream in the faith taught us from the Book of Books on our mother's knee, that our loved ones who have passed away are not gone from us forever, but that when our life-work is done we may meet them on "the other shore." But even if only a "myth" or "dream," I pray that no one may take away from me the comfort and solace which come from such a faith, unless he can give something better. But the Senator whose memory we honor to-day and millions of others who "have joined the redeemed" knew in whom they trusted; and the faith on which they so confidently leaned in life, I doubt not, has been realized beyond conception.

And now I add my garland to the wreath which we would twine in memory of him in whose honor we have turned aside. Honored Senator, faithful public servant useful citizen, beloved husband and father, farewell!

Address of Mr. CUTCHEON, of Michigan.

Mr. SPEAKER: Once more we stand in the presence of the great mystery of mysteries.

Death is the great mystery only because life is the greatest mystery of all.

Life is the one great, substantial thing; death, as we call it, is but the shadow. Life is activity, stir, worry, noise. Death comes and brings a pause, surcease from activity—quiet, silence.

I have stood in the midst of a New Hampshire manufacturing town, with its mile-long factories, and listened to the roar of its vast machinery, the clash-clash of its thousand looms, and the whirr of its million spindles. The day is verging to its close; the black columns of smoke roll up from the towering chimneys; the lights flash out from hundreds of windows; busy hands ply warp and woof and web, and restless feet fly hither and thither amidst the constant and unceasing roar.

Such, I said, is life!

It is full of rush and roar and clash and hurrying feet and flashing lights, and the web of life is rolled up from day to day and laid away.

But after a while there comes a sudden subsidence; the roar runs down through a minor cadence, and, with a moan, dies out. The clash of the thousand looms and the whirr of the million spindles cease; one by one the lights go out in the many rooms, and, with a shiver, the great mill stands still—dead.

Such is death. The machinery stops; the pulsation of the engine ceases; the lights are out; the windows are darkened. It is the resting of the brain, the folding of the hands, the stilling of the voice. It is the one, great, universal fact—the correlative of life.

The path of life may wind hither and thither, sometimes in the quiet of the valleys, "in the green pastures and beside the still waters;" sometimes over the storm-swept mountain heights, where tempests have beaten and frosts have seared and lightnings have scarred; sometimes by the quiet homestead on the hillside, and sometimes through camps and courts and palace halls; but wherever the path may wind throughout its progress it has but one ending—it comes at last to the door of a sepulcher.

One week ago we paused in our public duties to lay our garlands upon the tomb of Logan, the intrepid soldier, the impetuous orator, the fearless statesman, the honored Senator. To-day we linger for an hour to pay a willing tribute to one who was in all things his contrast. As Logan was a type of the new, strong, impulsive, ambitious West, so Senator PIKE was a good, substantial type of the older, staider, and more conservative spirit of the East. Logan brought with him the wind of the prairies, the mighty roll of the Mississippi, and the stormy voice of our great western inland seas. Our friend whom we mourn to-day bore about with him the quiet of his native New Hampshire valleys, and reflected in his life the placid flow of the lovely and romantic Merrimac or the bright unvexed lapse of the Pemigewasset. And yet he had in his character the solid and inflexible substratum of his own New Hampshire hills.

AUSTIN F. PIKE was a type and representative of the standard New England boy of the best class.

Address of Mr. Cutcheon, of Michigan. 85

Born to that most favorable lot for the development of manly character which entails neither grinding and pinching poverty upon the one hand nor wealth with its enervating luxuries and exemption from the necessity for effort upon the other, he grew up from childhood to know what it meant to work for whatever of comfort, competence, or education he possessed.

I never knew Senator PIKE personally until I met him here at the Capitol in December, 1883, but he was one of the very first of the Senators with whom I became acquainted. The fact that he came from the same county in which I was born and in which I spent all my boyhood days, and within whose soil sleep three generations of my ancestors, drew me strongly to him, and he greeted me with the warmth and heartiness of an old acquaintance.

His conversation was redolent of names and places and associations which were deeply woven into the woof and warp of my young life. It woke the slumbering memories of the years long gone as he talked of the hills and valleys of old Merrimac County, and the beautiful river of the same name, or the headlong Pemigewasset, which turned the busy mills of Franklin village, where the Senator spent most of his manhood life. Hard by, looking out over the green intervales, and shadowed by the great brooding trees, was the old Webster farm, where the great Daniel, whose fame as lawyer, statesman, and orator still stands unequaled in the great American pantheon, grew from boyhood to manhood.

Just here below the village is the little island which has been read of by almost every American school-boy of the last generation, where the heroic mother, Mrs. Dustin, slew her savage captors, in the early and troublous days of New England. To the westward, a few miles distant, old Kearsarge Mountain, a magnificent lift of primeval rock, with its bare back of uncovered granite, shoulders up against the clouds, the very picture and embodiment of "the everlasting hills."

Away to the north and east rose the towering summits of Washington and Adams and La Fayette, the solemn and majestic sentries of New Hampshire's northern frontier.

It was among scenes and associations like these that Senator PIKE spent all the days of his boyhood and manhood. Here he learned the gospel of work and the divine decree, "In the sweat of thy face shalt thou eat bread, till thou return unto the ground; for out of it wast thou taken: for dust thou art, and unto dust shalt thou return."

His youth was spent in the usual struggle of the New England boy for a living and an education.

The scanty and not over-fertile soil of New Hampshire, ground down from the upturned granite mountains by the frosts and snows, the suns and rains, the Titanic forces of a million years, does not yield its rewards except to hard blows and strenuous effort.

I believe it was Charles Mackay who said of the Western prairie that you can "tickle it with a hoe and it will laugh with a harvest." But it is not so with the rocky hills of New Hampshire. Sweat and back-ache are necessary fertilizers on her hill-side farms.

With steady step, however, he went forward from the school to the academy, from the academy to the college, thence reluctantly turning before his course was completed to the law office, where he came under the tuition of Judge

Nesmith, whose name in my boyhood days was linked with that of Webster as intimate friend and neighbor, and with whom afterward Senator PIKE became associated in the practice of the law.

Senator PIKE was first of all and above all a lawyer. He accepted public office as a duty, because his neighbors called him to it, and he felt that in this land, where the people rule and where the citizens must administer the affairs of state, every good citizen ought to contribute his share to the public weal by bearing his proportion in the labors, cares, and responsibilities of public station.

He was often called to office because he was trusted. His fellow-citizens had confidence in his fidelity, his industry, his intelligence, and his unswerving honesty. He first entered public official life in 1850, as a member of the State legislature, and in 1851 and 1852 as speaker of the house.

I well remember that in 1851, being then a pupil in the military institute in my native town of Pembroke, within sight of the capitol, I attended the opening of the legislature when Senator PIKE was first elevated to the office of speaker. How little I then dreamed, as I sat a boy in the gallery and saw him assume the gavel of the house, that after more than thirty years—most eventful years—we should meet in this Capitol. Little did I think that in that military school in the quiet valley of the Merrimac I was unconsciously preparing for the part I was to act in a very great drama upon a very wide stage. And yet the very next time I ever saw the late Senator was when we met in this Capitol, after the lapse of a generation, and after the tempestuous waves of a great war had swept over our land.

A few years later, in 1857 and 1858, Senator PIKE served

in the senate of his State, but without intermitting his practice of the law. His residence, only a score of miles from the capital and on the direct line of railroad communication, made it possible for him to serve the State and his large clientage at the same time.

Again, the people of his district claimed his service in the National Legislature in the Forty-third Congress, where he acquitted himself with credit.

In the memorable Senatorial contest of 1883, after a long and somewhat embittered struggle, the representatives of his State turned to him as the solution of their difficulties; and so he came to the national capital as United States Senator, as he had to the legislature of his State, not because he sought office but because he was willing to serve.

Of his service in the Senate I need not speak. He had scarcely completed the half of his term when he was called away. He was not conspicuous except for his sterling sense and his firmness and fidelity to duty as he understood it.

When he returned to the Senate in the Forty-ninth Congress he was conscious that the dread shadow was creeping over his life. He was weary and restless amid the gaieties and whirl of this capital, and he longed for sunny hills, the quiet nooks, the clear streams, and the green intervales of his own Merrimac valley.

He went back once more to look upon the friendly faces of the Sentinel Mountains, and to rest his tired body on the breast of the everlasting hills.

There, in the scenes of his boyhood, in the midst of the friends of his manhood years, patiently waiting while the shadow turned upon the dial of life, on the 8th of October last, at the age of sixty-seven years, he quietly, painlessly, passed through the shadow and into the brightness of the everlasting day.

Fit time to pass away.

The woods had put on the glory of the dying year; the birds of passage were seeking their Southern homes; the apples hung ripe in the orchard or fell over-ripe to the ground. The soft, dreamy haze of the evening of the year hung upon the distant hills, and all things admonished that it was the time of "the sere and yellow leaf." He passed with the passing year. Let us pause to-day and pay honor to the man of sterling qualities; the man who made his own way in the world by honest work; the man who commanded the confidence of his fellow-citizens; the man who rose by solid merit and enduring worth, step by step, to the highest office in the gift of the people of his State; the man true to his State, true to his friends, true to right.

Such a man was AUSTIN F. PIKE.

Mr. HAYNES. I now move the adoption of the resolutions.

The resolutions were unanimously agreed to; and accordingly, in pursuance of the last resolution, the House (at 4 o'clock and 35 minutes p. m.) adjourned.

www.ingramcontent.com/pod-product-compliance
Lightning Source LLC
Chambersburg PA
CBHW020259090426
42735CB00009B/1146